A Life in Three Motherlands
(Japan, Korea, USA)

A Life in Three Motherlands (Japan, Korea, USA)

You Can Do It!! I Did It—

Nancy Cantwell, RN, KNMW, CBE, LCT

Translated by Kana Sasaki
Edited by Sandra E. Elaissen

VANTAGE PRESS
New York

Contents

Introductory Remarks

Jo Leonard, MA, RN, FACCE,
Director of Parent Family Education

As the Director of St. Luke's Roosevelt Hospital Center's Parent Family Education Program I am pleased to share my impressions of Ms. Nancy Cantwell who has been an invaluable faculty member for almost twenty years. She recognized early on that her unique role as a Japanese-speaking registered nurse and childbirth educator could enable the hospital and the program to provide a previously nonexistent service to young Japanese families recently transferred to the New York metropolitan area. As a highly creative business woman and entrepreneur and—as one who truly understood the stresses of being in a foreign country, non-English speaking, pregnant, and without the support of family nearby—she developed the first hospital-sponsored childbirth education, baby care, and breastfeeding classes for Japanese families.

Nancy continued to challenge herself by producing a Japanese booklet and video to assist their understanding of childbirth and baby care. She also facilitated annual all-day reunion picnics for her families. Her popular columns in the New York Japanese newspapers were another resourceful method to promote education and responsible health care.

Although most families returned to Japan within two years, there is no doubt that many parents fondly remember "Miss Nancy" and the support and encouragement she provided them while in the United States. As someone with a foot in each cultural world, Nancy has been instrumental in promoting acceptance and understanding for the medical communities both in New York and in Japan. She has created opportunities for Japanese midwives to visit hospitals in New York, and she has gone to Japan to speak to midwives there. It is an honor and a privilege to know this talented and highly dedicated woman.

Jan Barger, RN, MA, IBCLC, RLC

Nancy and I "met" in November, 1993, when she enrolled in the Breastfeeding Support Consultant's (BSC) correspondence home study course. I was Nancy's instructor, and what a pleasure it was to get to know her through the mail. Completing the course, which was all in English, was a struggle for Nancy as she had to translate the written information into Japanese, write it all out in Japanese, and then translate it back into English. She was incredibly perseverant, however, and in February, 1997, we were able to send her well-earned and deserved certificate of completion. The course is a long one—it usually takes someone two years to complete it under the best of conditions. That Nancy was able to do it in just over three years is a testimony to her strong spirit.

Nancy feels that BSC taught her how to teach new mothers. She used to have childbirth education classes, breastfeeding classes, Baby and Mom classes, Junior baby classes, and grandmother classes in her home in Ft. Lee, New Jersey, for the many Japanese and some Korean mothers whose husbands are working for a short time in the United States, living in the New York area. Although she no longer teaches out of her home, she continues working with these mothers at St. Luke's Roosevelt Hospital in New York City, where she has been in the Family Education Department for the last twenty years. Many of these women feel like displaced persons, particularly having a baby in a very strange culture. Nancy is there for them, teaching and supporting them through this stressful time.

I was finally able to meet Nancy in person in 1997 when she attended BSC's on-site Lactation Education Program in the Philadelphia area. I felt as though I were meeting a dear friend! Nancy has taught me so much about the childbearing culture in Japan, as well as sharing bits and pieces of her most amazing life. I'm thrilled she has finally put it into writing; first in Japanese, and now in English.

Enjoy this book, and learn to love Nancy through its pages as I have.

Hiroshi Fujii, Educator

When Nancy asked me to write these comments for her autobiography, I was not sure if I was the right person for it. I decided to write this after giving it much thought, mainly because I realized that I have learned so much from the way she has lived her life. I would like to dedicate my words to Nancy for her devotion to life.

I am a son of Minoru Fujii, former director of the Hiroshima Sanatorium for wounded soldiers that Nancy talks about in the section of this book describing her life in Japan. I am the fourth and the youngest son among six children. It was around 1966 when I first saw the name of "Koh Namsun" on an envelope from Korea. I don't remember the details of her first letter, but I think she was asking my father to send her proof of her RN license in Japan and some textbooks about public health nursing. I was a college student then. I didn't have good feelings toward Korea because of the political relations between Japan and Korea. Following the signing of the Japan-Korea Fundamental Agreement in 1965, and having insufficient knowledge of the Agreement, I joined some demonstrations against it. And I was also opposed to Korea's military dictatorship. Under such circumstances, I was very interested in the letter from Korea, written in beautiful Japanese calligraphy. Ever since, my interest in and positive feelings towards Korea have grown strongly through her letters.

She described her life so vividly in her letters. I was deeply moved by her survival spirit. I soon found myself looking forward to receiving her letters to my father.

When her letters started coming from America instead of Korea, she described not only the hardship of her life, but also her hopes. The theme of these letters was that one's efforts would definitely be rewarded someday. She wrote how hard her life was: "Why do I have to suffer so much?"; "I live my life on a hand-to-mouth basis 24 hours a day"; "I am concerned about my children's education." But we also received bright news such as "I bought land in Florida"; "My daughter entered the university"; "My son joined the army." In the meantime, I married and my father moved in with us in Hiroshima after he retired from the hospital, where he had worked for thirty-five years. In all those years, her letters from New York have been giving me and my family energy to live on.

Although I knew her through her letters, I had never met her until March 1977, when I accompanied my parents on their visit to America. We visited New York and I met her for the first time. We went to the Empire State Building together. As we stood on the observatory deck of the building, looking down at Manhattan, she said "When I drive a car in New York, I think about myself working in this big city. That gives me a lot of courage." I was very impressed by her way of life.

In addition to working as a nurse, she attempted anything that brought her extra income, including selling Royal Jelly tablets. And using her midwife license, she started a Lamaze class. My father was falling ill; his heart condition worsened. But he was very happy to hear that Namsun was helping many young Japanese mothers to give birth in America. He continued to read her letters over and over as if he were a proud father as she succeeded in America. She wrote in one letter, "Even I have the right to be happy." She told us of changing her name to Nancy and about her new life with Larry, her American husband. My father was surprised at her words "right to be happy" and was very happy for her new start.

We finally met Larry when Nancy and Larry visited Japan in 1980. My father was very impressed with Larry and happy for Nancy, saying, "wonderful gentleman" of Larry when he saw how humorous he was and how considerate he was of Nancy. My father died in August 1989. In March of that year he was hospitalized in Hiroshima Hospital for a broken backbone. I cannot forget that Nancy went out of her way to visit my father at the hospital then.

I am getting closer to retirement. From my college years to present, letters from Ms. Koh Namsun/Nancy taught me "I should make more effort" and "my efforts will be rewarded someday." She has lived her life in three different countries—first as a Japanese, then as a Korean, and finally as an American. She has lived her life using her talent and endless effort. It is not something ordinary people can do.

In February 2002, I was sitting with her in the living room in her New Jersey apartment, looking at the Manhattan skyline across the Hudson River. As soon as she told me of her plan to publish her autobiography, I was very excited and encouraged her. I offered my help and my ability. I am very happy that she finally has published this book. I hope that it will give courage to its readers, as it did to me.

Preface

I live in a beautiful condominium building in Fort Lee, New Jersey, and the view from our eleventh-floor apartment is breathtaking. The living room overlooks the harbor of New York City from the George Washington Bridge to the Empire State Building. We used to see the beautiful twin buildings of the World Trade Center. Night views are magnificent, with different colored illuminations and the lights of the halogen lamps on the bridge. For nearly twenty years, I have enjoyed those views with my wonderful and very handsome Irish-American husband, the man of my dreams.

With my husband, Larry, in Fort Lee, New Jersey

People say "life is short," but in retrospect, I have had a long although difficult life in all three motherlands, Japan, Korea, and America. I faced economic and language problems in each country, and the devastation of World War II in Japan, the Korean War in the early 1950s, and, here in America, the horror of September 11, 2001. Finally, however, I found an exceptional interracial love as a woman in my fifties and we have had a successful marriage for twenty-five years. I believe that I wouldn't be as grateful as I am now, had my earlier years not been so troubled.

A Life in Three Motherlands
(Japan, Korea, USA)

One
Japan

Childhood in Osaka

I was born in Osaka, Japan, near the Nagara River. I am not sure whether my family owned or rented, but our two-story house was not a very nice one. A large lumberyard was adjacent to this house, but the piled up logs were used by the neighborhood children as a playground from morning until sunset, when everyone went home. The Takedas, a well-to-do family, lived in a beautiful home across the road and the youngest daughter, Ochino-San, was one of my close playmates. In the evenings, the Takedas' maid would call out, *"Ojo-San! Gohan de suyo!"* (Young lady: dinner's ready!) It was time for all of us to go home our separate ways.

Ochino and the others were playground friends only: that is, I was always excluded on holidays such as New Year's and *Hina-matsuri*, the national girl's day on March 3rd. The other children were always invited to the Takedas' for holiday celebrations, when they wore lovely kimonos with long sleeves, played Japanese card games, and were served delicious food. I used to peek into the Takedas' house through a hole in the entrance gate and I envied them so much. As I left the gate, I developed the habit of whispering abusive language to vent all my frustrations. As a small child, I got along well with these friends—except for the natural quarrels children have—but when we did argue, they always taunted me, calling me, "Korean," or "squint eye." Being a youngster, I really didn't understand what they meant, although I sensed that something was wrong; and, of course, what was wrong was the racism that was felt toward Koreans. In our national clothing, we readily appeared different. My mother wore the *chima* and *chogori*, the traditional Korean costume, rather than kimonos, which are the tradition among Japanese. She also spoke Korean and she talked to me in broken Japanese with a Korean accent. I wished she would wear a kimono and I so resented and blamed her for my playmate's prejudices.

When I was three years old, my right eye had been struck by a sharp object. My poor mother was terribly frightened and, because she had so little education, mistakenly took me to an acupuncturist instead of an ophthalmologist. The injury I sustained became permanent—a squint and an almost complete loss of vision in that eye. I have never overcome the trauma of blindness or the pain of exclusion.

My family originated from Korea, where my father was born on Cheju Island. He had emigrated to Osaka in the early twentieth century and seemed to be doing well by helping fellow Koreans find jobs and boarding houses. He even owned a house and farmland in Korea, hoping to return in glory one day, but his dream ultimately brought unimaginable grief to our family. I remember the chores I did as a little girl to help him, washing a lot of rice with my small hands and lots of dishes as well. I had a brother, Nam Hak, thirteen years older than I, and a sister, Nam Bong, six years older. Nam Hak graduated from high school, but my sister was not permitted to go because of her gender. She was forced to work during the day in factories and studied writing and reading secretly at night. Luckily, time civilized my father to some extent and I was allowed to go to school.

Until I began elementary school, everyone called me by a nickname, Kinoko (I don't know what it means), but on entering school, my registered name, Namsun Koh, which was chosen by my father, was used publicly. The meaning of my formal name is "declaration higher in the south." In school, my grades were not so bad, although it is true that I preferred playing outside to studying in the classroom. I have a rather unpleasant memory of one experience, for one day when I was a first-grade student, I played in the schoolyard during the mid-class break. The bell rang and the next class began. I went into the classroom, but as soon as the lesson started, I needed to use the restroom. I was embarrassed, but nevertheless asked the teacher if I could be excused. When I returned to class, the door was locked and the teacher handed me a chair through the window, saying, "Sit in front of the shrine and think about what you just did." I sat at the shrine in a corner of the schoolyard for a full forty-five minutes until the class ended. The schoolyard I had thought to be too small when I played there with my friends suddenly seemed much too big. When my classmates came out afterward, I was so ashamed and hid my face with my arm in mortification! I still remember this incident as another early traumatic event.

Days at Onomichi

Both Nam Hak and Nam Bong were married in Osaka, and my parents moved the family to a small village called Samba near Onomichi in the Hiroshima prefecture. I was in third grade and by then had another sister, Nam Gi, six years younger than I. I was transferred to a new and smaller school in this rural area. There were no other Korean students besides me, but I didn't sense any bigotry. It was a small seaside village with beautiful ever-green mountains behind it and I grew up so freely surrounded by the beauties of nature. I often went up into the mountains with my friends and collected pine needles and pine cones. It was so quiet—the only sounds being the chirping of the birds. Sometimes we sang Japanese folk songs and when we lost each other, our singing voices led us back. My memories too are of gathering firewood, bundling and binding the needles and cones, and bringing them home to sell or use in our own homes. From a distance we appeared to be many bundles of pine shrubs moving on small legs. As the lyrics say, " . . . the dream still circles round me—unforgettable, my homeland."

My parents had rented a house of only two rooms, where they and I lived. I worked on my lessons using a cardboard box as my study desk, but when I studied I used the dining room table. The small kitchen was near the entrance, but we didn't have water pipes, so my chore was to make a daily trip, passing the railroad tracks to bring water from a well. The house, although very small, faced the ocean. When the tide was high, we could actually fish from our little veranda, and when low, we were able to collect seaweed and shellfish for our dinners. Winters brought us heavy snows and I think with pleasure of the "early morning gathering" that was held every year during school vacation. A horn was blown while it was still dark outside and I was awakened, bundled into warm clothes and sent to join the other children at the village gathering place where a bonfire blazed. After all the villagers were present, the fire was doused and, following the "leader" and shouting "*Yoisha, Yoisha,*"we ran to the schoolyard, praying at the shrine on our way. This tradition was followed by game playing in the schoolyard with other village groups; by the time the sun rose, our spirits were high, our breath steaming, and our faces red. Our games ended, the groups dispersed, and we returned to our homes. It was only a simple event, but it remains a fond memory.

I enjoyed sports as a student, learning the Japanese martial art, "*naginata*" (a long-sword activity) and playing dodge ball and volleyball. In our white, neat costumes, our volleyball team managed to lose the tournaments, having never defeated another school as far as I remember. Onomichi was famous for cultivating big, tasty peaches, so, in summer, one of our school sports was swimming and hunting for the peaches thrown into the ocean by the village farmers. I was a good swimmer, competing in a 3,000 meter race along the shore and I was one of the remaining eight after all the others had dropped out. I also recall when the ferry, "*Toyo-maru,*" passed our shore and, shouting "*Toyoja, Toyoya,*" we threw off our school clothes, diving into the sea, wearing only our undergarments. The wake of the ferry provided waves of various types and sizes, which surely added to our fun. Swimming was a pastime I learned naturally, although I never anticipated that my skill would later help in teaching pregnant women about the different pain "waves" they would undergo in labor.

I was a good student with a satisfactory record and I especially had fun acting in a number of roles in school plays at the annual school arts festivals, once playing an evil, nursing mother in a famous samurai story of the *Edo* period (*Ohoka Echizen*). In that role, the evil and hardened woman was found guilty, so I wonder if I gave my peers the impression that I was tough even then. There is no doubt, however, that all these childhood experiences affected my personality in the years and decades ahead.

Among many friends, I especially remember one transferred student, Yayoi Tokunaga, the only daughter of the president of an ice manufacturing company. With her attractive face and sophistication, Yayoi became the center of everyone's attention in our small village. She and I often played together in the office of her family's business and we became good friends. We even bathed together in her big *Goemon*-style bath. She was one friend who didn't discriminate because I was Korean and I hold the image of our bathing as a warm recollection to this day.

One day I took Yayoi to an inlet next to her house to teach her how to swim. She could not stay afloat at all and she grabbed me in desperation, both of us sinking into the deep water. I don't remember how we got out, but that my thoughts at the time were to save Yayoi under any circumstances. I told myself that even if I died, I needed to protect this only, precious child of an important man, for her life was important and mine was not. I met Yayoi fifty years later and we are still good friends, bound together by this incident, although the Pacific Ocean and a continent are between us.

Upon graduating, Yayoi and most of my other friends entered a middle school, but because my family couldn't afford the tuition there, I remained at elementary school for an extra two-year curriculum. In eighth grade I was designated "honcho" (group leader) of the school's cleaning crew. Back then, I thought that we should really work hard because I certainly wouldn't die of the work. This became my catchphrase and I did my very best to clean the facility, working alongside the other cleaners. The hard work was eventually rewarded by the principal, and I was honored with a special award for effort. That catchword became a life-long formula: after sixty years, I still think of it as the symbol of my heart and my lifestyle.

It was at that stage of my life that my father and brother were partners in a steamboat business, bringing metal wastes from a shipyard on Mukai Island and selling the waste to make a living. My brother continued to operate the business on his own after my father died of stomach cancer at the time World War II was intensifying. At school, foods such as pickled plums were collected from each household; on the streets of the village, women wearing the white aprons and cords of the national defense organization asked the public to help in making a one-thousand-stitch *hachimaki* (a bandana-like textile to wrap around one's head) for each of the soldiers who were going off to the war. A thousand people were enlisted in this project and I gathered pine leaves and cones in the mountains, selling them to earn money as donations to the defense fund. I was proud of my ability to contribute. Looking back, it seemed such an innocent act. As the war progressed women began wearing air defense hats and pants instead of skirts, taking part in air defense drills and training with bamboo spears. None of the shops sold food or daily necessities: everything was provided through a rationing system, a circulating bulletin informing the public when supplies would arrive.

Even at school more time was spent in the play yard on war training than on academic study and, occasionally, we were sent to the rice fields rather than classes to help the farmers. In return, the farmers fed us rice balls made with rich white rice: I can never forget how delicious they were. Many students were mobilized for the war effort, forced to work in factories and live in boarding houses apart from our families. If you passed by, you could hear the sound of a plaintive ballad that all the youngsters sang: "I visited a boy's room with my pillow. One o'clock in the morning. Hold me. Night is deep. The moon is above the roof of the factory." I still sing this song from time to time and realize that the war was not a dream.

One day, I had a chance to see the movie, *Hospital Ship*, which affected me a great deal so I decided to be a nurse. The theme was of a Japanese Red Cross nurse in wartime, treating wounded soldiers aboard even though she suffered from motion sickness herself. I was deeply moved by her sacrifice and determination. Eventually, I applied to the Red Cross Nursing School. At the time, I had to pass the three-day-long exam to enter this school, but I was rejected on the very first day because my blind right eye affected my field of vision. I was excluded from both the oral as well as written tests, and I wept in disappointment constantly for many days.

In the meanwhile, the day for an examination at the Sanatorium for Returning Veterans was also drawing closer and I was very concerned about my blind eye. Nevertheless, I passed the physical, and the oral and written exams were not so difficult. I wasn't as excited as I expected to be when I received the letter of notification that I had passed these exams because I had failed in my application to the Red Cross School. Yet, as the first day of classes approached, I was able to put my failure aside. In fact, it was fortunate that I had failed at my original application: the rejection probably saved my life! *Hospital Ship* was a young girl's romantic dream, but the reality was far different. Had I succeeded, I would have been the first nurse to be sent to the battlefield simply because of my nationality—Koreans were expendable and I would have died there in no time. There is a saying, "If you have lost something, you will get something else instead." I believe it. I was later told that I passed the Veteran's Hospital entrance exam in second place. As the first-place student did not enter the school, I was officially first in my class among sixty-two applicants.

Nursing School

Entrance to nursing school

It took about two hours by slow train for my sister Nam Bong and me to reach Saijo station from Onomichi and when I arrived, I found a nurse awaiting me. To my surprise, there had been six or seven other entrants on the same train. The nurse, a third-year student, dressed in white hat, uniform, socks, and shoes introduced herself and called our names one by one from the list she held, directing us to follow her while she kept up a quick pace on the rough mountain roads. She reminded me of the nurse in *Hospital Ship*, and I daydreamed of becoming like her in the future, which excited me as we neared the school. Other young girls, accompanied by their parents or guardians, must have been having similar dreams of the future, and of becoming a nurse. After we had been walking close to an hour, hospital buildings appeared here and there and we finally entered the gate marked "Hiroshima Veteran's Hospital." It was a 40.8–acre parcel of land on which thirteen wooden wards held about 1,200 beds. In the hills beyond the wards were small cottages for recovering patients. The new students were taken to *Shirahato-ryo* (White Dove Dorm) a two-story structure near the main hospital building.

When I saw my name, Namsun Koh, on the door of my room on the second floor and on my foot locker, I was exhilarated to realize that I really had passed the exam and was becoming a nursing student. I shared this little room with new students, Aiko Kawazoe and Shizuko Daii, and the room "chief," Suzue Hiraki, two years ahead of us. The room held a small cabinet, which we shared, and a small desk for each of us. In winter, an inadequate brazier was used for warmth, but it was a far better environment than my own home. I felt so happy, as if I were living in a palace. No! It was better than a palace.

Every morning, although still dark, the wake-up bell was rung and we had fifteen minutes to dress before roll call.

"Report from Room Number 3. Count! One, two, three. Three plus the room chief. All are accounted for."

After Ms. Ishikura, the nursing director, took attendance, she led us to the temple to pray. There, the new student's role was to read the nurses' oath aloud: "Seniors lead juniors with kindness; Juniors follow their lead,"etc. Our morning ritual must have been quite a sight for the convalescent men. Prayers were followed by breakfast and the smell of steamed rice filled the kitchen. Our menu never varied: a small portion of rice, two pieces of *takuwan* (pickled radish), and miso soup made with very few ingredients. It was actually a rather rich breakfast for such a period of food shortages.

All the patients were soldiers who had been discharged from active service, although nurses had to behave as though in the military as well. When I came across senior students in the hallway, I had to stop at once, bow, and say, *"Otsukare sama de gozaimasu,"* that is, "You must be tired from your hard work." Their responses were different, and dependent on the individual senior. Nice ones would smile back at me, but those who were not agreeable would either fail to reply or would ignore my presence altogether. Had I ever neglected to acknowledge them, I would have become the object of their scorn and malice.

Walking to the pharmacy one morning, I saw Dr. Fujii, the principal, walking in my direction and I became very edgy because of his status and also because he was known to be the type of intense individual who made people nervous. I was certain that if I behaved incorrectly, my grades would be affected. I stopped immediately and bowed with my most profound respect.

"Oh, hello," was his smiling response. "Working hard?" My tension melted. I was amazed at his kind and friendly attitude. How could I know then that he would be so great a source of support throughout my life?

A month into the new semester, we, the new students, began to actually look like nurses, in our white uniforms altered to fit and our starched hats. Starching was not an easy task to perform. I had to sacrifice my meal, or if I was lucky, use rice left over by patients without an appetite, but in any event, I needed a cup of steamed rice to starch a set of uniforms. The starched hat was spread on the window glass so I wouldn't have to iron it. This starch battle aside, everything

I did at school was great fun and I think one reason for my pleasure was that all the patients were male veterans ages eighteen to thirty. It was exciting for a young woman like myself to see these young men even if they were ill. They seemed very nice and often amusing.

Working on the Wards

浴氣外ルケ於ニ室歌都
(所療療島廣人工球傷)

Resting time

For the new students, working on the wards meant cleaning the building's facilities, patient's mucus, replacing gargling cups and bed pans, distributing large kettles filled with hot water to patients taking their medications, and serving tea at meal times. I used to wonder when I would be allowed to note patients' conditions on their charts or accompany doctors on their rounds. Nevertheless, I enjoyed everything assigned to me, and was careful to follow the strict regulations that governed conversing with the patients: the seniors were ever watchful to enforce this prohibition.

Many patients sympathized with my strenuous work schedule and said so. Indeed, I did work hard. A day came when I was called to the office of the head nurse. Naturally I was fearful because such a summons was usually not a promising sign—I might have done something wrong. I wasn't sure. I entered with trepidation until I saw the smile on her face and realized that it might be quite the opposite.

"I want to give you a temporary name. You will soon be dealing directly with more and more patients and I think that working with them might be easier if you have a name that sounds Japanese. She handed me a new name tag reading "Minami Koh." At the time I was relieved and very appreciative of her kindness and concern.

Announcements were sometimes a special occasion, such as the night there was a roll call for the entire student body. I was shocked when I heard the head nurse read my name. Apparently, she had been sent a thank-you letter from the representative of the patients in Ward 12. It was the first such letter they had ever received from patients. I was extremely happy and proud to hear the announcement and credited this success to my image of the screen nurse and my catchphrase to work hard, the promise I had made to myself in the eighth grade.

I had favorites among my classes and preferred the stretcher drill with Drill Sergeant Toda. We learned the technique for turning a stretcher and CPR to be used in the frontlines, military training that wasn't taught in ordinary schools. But I also enjoyed the annual recreation party for hospital staff and patients that was held on the 5th of January. It was a kind of talent show among us, some dancing to Japanese folk songs, some acting the role of characters in a famous ghost story, and once, dressed as a man, I danced to the song,

"I am a sailor." These are the joyful days that have remained in my thoughts. There are less pleasant recollections of my student days, such as the shortages of necessities during the war and having to write on previously printed cookie box wrappings, which I bought with the minimal spending money we earned for our hospital labor. In order to correspond with my family, I used the reverse sides of the paper for letter writing, and then folded these sheets into envelopes. We all had to "make do."

Active-Duty Wards

As the war continued, wounded marines began arriving from the battlefields. Soon, the hospital was treating not only discharged soldiers, but also marine officers in active service. The name of the hospital was changed to Marine Hospital Hiroshima Sanatorium. Chisome Shimokubo and I were always assigned together to the active-duty ward—it seems I was in demand because of my attitude and personality. In this ward, officers and staff lived as though aboard warships: for example, the early morning wake-up call. While it was still dark, standing in front of the nurse's station, I had to shout aloud, "Everyone UP! Five minutes to reveille!" In the marines, everything is commanded with five-minute lead time, but I was nervous conducting the prior call as though I were in the service as well. Worse, I then had to shout aloud, "Everyone up!" With this command, all the patients rose and prepared for roll call and tidying their beds. In this ward, unlike others, the patients were assigned certain chores, even mopping and scrubbing the hospital floor just as they would do were they on deck. This chore also began with a command: "Washing the deck in five minutes!"

One morning, I observed a very odd interchange: a forty-two-year-old marine, who had been conscripted, was scrubbing the floor, his hospital robe tucked in on his back. An eighteen-year-old marine enlistee, who was supervising and carrying a baton called "the military-discipline spirits stick" addressed him, "Soldier Yamada."

The older man stopped scrubbing at once, stood up straight, then answered, "Yes sir."

The young man responded, "Don't you want to eat these cookies, Yamada?" holding up the old sealing paper from the cookie box the older man had bought at the hospital commissary. Yamada answered, "Yes sir. I would like to eat them, sir." The brief conversation about some cookies and conducted in military fashion was truly bizarre, especially during the misfortune of war-time conditions. Here were two men hardened for combat, simply intent on nibbling sweets.

Military discipline was taken very seriously at the hospital, where opportunities arose for strange incidents. One such situation took place when a patient developed a fever of 40 degrees C. The Chief Marine, Mizutani, the patient representative, visited him and put his hand on the patient's forehead, asking, "Are you all right?" Instantly, Mizutani's face became stony and he screamed out my name, "Nurse Koh, can you take his temperature once again? And please stay with him while it is registering." I placed the thermometer under the patients armpit and waited three minutes. It read 36 degrees C. Normal temperature. The patient confessed later that he had rubbed the thermometer against his blanket to raise the temperature while the nurses were at other bedsides. Angered, Mizutani, discipline stick in hand, ordered the patient out into the yard barefoot. He then beat the malingerer in full view of the other patients and staff with the stick until the patient lost consciousness. "Watch closely," he announced. "Japan's marines are losing the war because of soldiers like you!" he said, pouring a bucket of water on him. "You lack the military spirit!" A military doctor came to stop Mizutani, but was too late to prevent the patient from developing a real fever. The incident had a profound effect on my image of the military.

Food shortages were a severe problem, as the hospital had to provide for 1,200 staff members and patients. I cannot begin to imagine the concern of the hospital's director, Dr. Minoru Fujii. Fortunately, the hospital was surrounded by mountains and ringed by huge tracts of farmland—we nurses had to feed ourselves from what we farmed on hospital grounds. Some nurses from farmers' families would go home and return with rice or rice cake, which they cooked in tin cans on the small brazier, but the aroma of steaming rice only deepened the sense of starvation in the others. I was assigned to the farming group growing vegetables for the hospital, and each participant was given two potatoes as a reward for our labor. I didn't mind farming even though it was hard work, and the potatoes tasted so special! Potatoes have never tasted as good since.

Food shortages! Three key elements in the treatment of tuberculosis (TB) are nutrition, air, and rest, according to Dr. Fujii, and we were lacking the most important, nutrition. In order to supplement our meager provisions, a pond called Oswada, on hospital land, and filled with fish, was drained and we were able to eat the carp for dinner—at least for a little while. The carp smelled like mud, but supplied the necessary nutrients to our patients.

Many patients escaped from the hospital during the night to go to nearby farms where they stole leaves of radish and cooked on small electric ranges hidden under their beds. The meals they cooked with the radish leaves, a lot of water, soy sauce, and a small amount of rice which they got from their dinner was a very watery porridge, but their escapes and hidden ranges were an open secret everyone knew and ignored. I received a letter once from a former patient who wrote that he used "to bear the terrible hunger by eating that cat's-vomit-like gruel." It was a bitter joke, but reminded me of how hungry we all were. Yet I still feel nostalgic when I think of it! Besides the secret ranges, the ward had no heating system, although giving patients hot water bottles was a nurse's job. In the "boiler" room, patients who weren't seriously ill helped us to boil water and there were a few rumors of love matches between nurses and patients. Unfortunately, I didn't personally experience any.

I have mentioned Dr. Fujii many times. He had come to this hospital in 1939 as a young director in his thirties, and he dedicated his life to helping patients. I didn't have much direct contact with him. However, I knew he was a strict, but kind leader. After I left Japan for Korea, and then the United States, I continued to correspond with him and tell him of my new life. He was always so thoughtful in answering my letters and encouraging me. I cannot explain how much these letters supported me through the years. I believe that I am here, in America, living my life as I am now, because of him and his warmth; he was like my spiritual father. He passed away many years ago. I pray for his soul.

The war was intensifying day by day and it was not surprising at all to see air battles near the hospital itself. It was like watching a film and I had no fear. About that time, our white uniforms were discontinued and we wore the military colors. We also began hearing sirens indicating attack warnings. Each time we heard the warning sirens, we moved our patients to the shelter and in each ward, two nurses were selected to report these evacuations to Dr. Fujii. Shimokubo and I were always assigned the task of specifying the ward and the number of its patients. Wearing the messenger arm bands we were given, she and I ran through the dark hallways to the room referred to as "headquarters," where the windows were covered with drapes, black outside and red inside. At headquarters, Dr.Fujii, other doctors, and management personnel awaited our report. We stood directly in front of them and barked out, "Shimokubo reporting. Ward Number 6. There were forty-two patients altogether; two having gone home. Therefore, at the moment, we have forty. We have five nurses on reporting assignment." Shimokubo returned to her ward and my mission was to remain at headquarters to bring the all-clear to the wards later on. I sat in a corner feeling very uncomfortable in the presence of my superiors. Now, this seems so unreal to me.

Hiroshima

Because the war was worsening every day, graduation was held early, in July 1945–whether fortunately or unfortunately, I didn't know. On August 6, one month later, the United States dropped the atomic bomb on Hiroshima and shook the world.

Remembering

Fifty years later I attended a reunion of my old nursing school companions. When I entered the room that first time, I saw a group of strange old ladies; but I soon realized that the image in my mind of girls in the bloom of youth was only that, an image. Those youngsters, including me, had faded many, many years earlier.[1]

I asked my classmates to relate their experiences when the bomb fell. I was interested in their viewpoints and how they may have differed from my own. I taped their conversations, as transcribed below:

Kaneko: I was working a night shift and finished up in the morning. It was a beautiful morning—not a cloud in an endless blue sky. I was watching a B-29 flying over the hospital early and repeatedly. I was watching from the window with other nurses and commenting that a yellow alert had not been raised. I commented that we need not worry because

---

[1] A conversation among my classmates and myself recounts our experiences at Hiroshima.

23

the hospital had the Red Cross insignia and the enemy would not attack a hospital. I went about my tasks, cleaning the exam rooms, and it was then that something suddenly flashed.

Nancy: What time was that? (I wanted to make sure that my memory of the time was correct.)

All the women answered simultaneously: Around 8:15.

Kaneko: It was a huge flash. Dr Fujii in the pharmacy asked, "Who has been playing with a mirror."

All laughed.

Tsuyaka: Patients always played with mirrors from the ward window and at the moment we saw the flash, no one yet knew of its terrible consequences, except for the Americans who had dropped the bomb.

Kaneko: Then it was booooooom! And afterward, the attack warning. I think I looked out of the window and saw three big clouds in the sky. As I said, "The parachutes are coming down," the clouds grew bigger and bigger.

Tsuyaka: It looked just like a fist and it was all white.

Hiroko: I said, "What is that? Did Kaita gas tank blow up?" Then, at about 10:30 A.M., we heard that Hiroshima had been bombed.

Kaneko: Senior nurses organized a rescue team and left as soon as the news came in. There were so many wounded brought in after 2:00 P.M. that day. The first patients had injuries they received driving to Hiroshima following the explosion, when they crashed into a train. It demonstrated that everyone was in a state of panic during the attack, a panic too terrible to watch.

Satoko: Terue San, didn't all your family die in the attack?

Terue: Yes, they did. Only my older sister survived. When I went to the city as a member of the rescue team, I looked for my family, but our house was gone and my relations were gone. I sat on the street and burst out crying. It was terrible.

(But even so terrible a memory seems to be fading after fifty years.)

Sachiko: I went to Hiroshima the day after the bomb was dropped. I was on a truck and as we neared Kaita City, we felt the burning heat. We drove into Hiroshima and there were still many people walking around with their charred skin hanging from their bodies. At this point, I still did not know that it had been an atomic bomb, so wasn't sure of what I was seeing and I thought that I, too, would die soon. I was so frightened. From the next day on, every time I checked the patients at night, I found six or seven already dead. Their burnt and swollen faces were all bandaged, so it was actually hard to tell who was still alive and who was dead. I was too frightened to touch them, but if they were dead, we had to take the bodies to a charnel in the mountain.

Satoko: I still feel that I can smell the stench.

Akiko: I was working at the lab, so all I did was count patients' blood cells. Everyone's white cells were decreasing day by day; it was our Dr. Shirai who first found the victims whose white cells had been destroyed.

Nancy: It was said that grass would not grow in Hiroshima for at least seven years.

Rescue

I was assigned to join the third-day rescue team and headed to Hiroshima on a truck. As soon as we arrived, I became nauseated from the indescribable smell and the smoke that remained here and there. We were supposed to go to the gym of a school where patients had been brought, but entering the gym I was assaulted by the sickening odor. I almost screamed and ran away, for there was such horror before my eyes. Here it was, seventy-two hours after the explosion, but the gym was filled with patients who had not been treated at all because of the destruction the bomb caused everywhere. These were burn victims whose faces were black and swollen. There was no way to determine their gender by simply looking at them. Some wore white running shirts at the time of the bombing and the skin that had been covered by the shirts was clean. Many dead bodies lay among the still living, but no one was able to object to the corpses next to them.

We, the rescue team, prepared buckets of olive oil mixed with zinc oxide powder and painted the burnt bodies using brushes to apply the mixture. Fearfully, I picked up a victim's skin with tweezers. It was an awfully hot August and I was mortified to find tons of maggots growing there; the abundance of human protein available as food was encouraging their rapid growth. I wanted to cry and vomit right then, but instead, I took the maggots away with the tweezers, cleansed the area, applied disinfectant, and painted on the zinc oil treatment. It was hard to believe that maggots were living under the skin of live human bodies; I had never heard of it before and there were a huge number of patients in the same condition. Someone came up with the idea of hosing the maggots off the bodies with clean water. I was weeping inside, but had to work calmly.

Soon after, other rescue groups arrived and some food was provided. Rice balls were still tasty although the dreadful stench spread throughout the entire city. I had to wonder, though, about where this food came from. So much food was donated and delivered to us, but it was supposed to be a time of great shortages. We weren't supposed to have that much food! I thought about how hungry we had been every day and I became angry. While we suffered, there was food some-where: where that was, we didn't know.

As evening fell, the rain began. We climbed back on our truck, returning to the hospital. It was already night when I saw many blue fire balls, burning phosphorus in the dark air. Frightened that the spirits of the dead were coming to haunt me, I held my head low, my knees tight against my chest, but I couldn't stop shivering. I have never been so frightened before or since.

Many burn victims were rushed to our hospital. Other patients who had been there and were recovering well enough helped the nurses to care for these newly injured One bomb victim came in with both hands burnt, his skin and nails all hanging together, his face completely bandaged. "It hurts. It hurts," he repeated as he wandered, leaving a river-like track. Spreading along the floor, were his precious body fluids. When I arrived the next day, he was dead, dehydrated among other injuries.

Now we were facing a shortage of medical supplies. There was not enough gauze, so we alternated with other cloths as well as newspaper. I don't think that the use of newspaper to replace gauze for dressings was simply my imagination. A month later, the hospital began receiving other types of bomb victims: patients who had not been di-rectly exposed to the thermal effects of the nuclear weapon. These people were rapidly losing their white blood cells, bleeding from their gums, and needing blood transfusions. Many healthy people, including me, donated blood, particu-larly because we were well fed in return.

War's End; A New Journey

World War II officially ended on August 15, 1945. Many wept as they listened to the Emperor's voice on the radio. The public had never heard his voice before and his speech was repeated over and over. Many knew that this day would come, but some patients coughed up blood from the shock. Some patients died because their conditions worsened after the war was lost. All soldiers who had shaved heads began regrowing their hair. Originally dedicated solely to military men, the hospital began to treat female patients as well.

Not long after the armistice, I remember being called to the office of the director of nursing. She handed me a letter. It was from my brother and was addressed to her, but informed me that he was returning to Korea because the war had ended. I didn't want to leave Japan or the hospital, but it immediately seemed my duty to return also. I was saddened that my exciting and joyous life at the hospital was over. I wished that my brother had never existed. In retrospect, as an autonomous woman I had the right to decide to stay or to leave, and I regret I didn't know it then.

Because my return to Korea was a consequence of the war's end, Dr. Fujii gave me special permission so that I could graduate from nursing school and receive a nursing license early, in spite of needing more practical training. I cannot stress well enough how that piece of paper, my license, helped me survive throughout my life, nor can I adequately express my gratitude to that good man. It was a time of misery for Japan after losing the war, and Dr. Fujii must have realized how very much I would need something to stand on in order to survive.

I went "home" to Onomichi with my nursing license. There, I learned that my brother had no immediate plans for returning to Korea. I thought, "No. I don't want to go back to Korea. I don't even speak the Korean language. What will I do there? I finally have my license, but it will be worthless there." Still, I thought it was too late to change the future and I couldn't go back to school. After long consideration, I decided to register with a private nursing association and I worked as a private nurse until we left for Korea.

My first private nursing patient was an elderly man who had had a stroke. He lived in an old farmhouse in the mountains. I don't remember the exact location, although I do recall that it took me two days to reach him. The house didn't have a well but the clean mountain water flowed through a bamboo pipe that led from that beautiful natural setting to the house, and served their needs for kitchen, bath, and even a pond. There was a continuous supply of clear, fresh water available, in contrast with my own house in Onomichi, where I had to go to the well with two buckets. In the big cities, everyone competed in order to live, but my patient and his family were warm and simple people. I'm always amazed when I think back on how much those farmers ate!

I had a few more cases before my brother decided to sail to Korea along with our belongings. Koreans were legally permitted to return by ship from Shimonoseki City in Japan, but there was a limit of 500 yen per person that one could take out of Japan and our luggage was limited to two pieces per passenger. Nam Hak wanted to take all we had and his choice was a black market boat; that was how the four members of his family, my mother, my younger sister, Nam Gi, and I traveled across the Korean Strait. To tell the truth, I had a small secret I hadn't revealed to anyone at the time about a young man, Iwao Miyamoto. My recollection isn't exactly perfect, but I know that he was a patient representative of the 12th Ward at the Marine Hospital. I didn't realize it then, but I was thinking about him a lot. We had sometimes spoken of personal matters and I learned that his parents were no longer alive; he did, however, still have a sister. That was all I knew, but I wanted to know more. He and I became pen pals when I left the hospital, and in one letter I received, he wrote of our future together. At that point in my life, corresponding with him was my only passion and I was despondent that our friendship would be over if I went back to Korea. Two days before sailing I told my older sister about him and asked her to help me.

She, however, had problems of her own. Her husband, a conscripted soldier, was still out of the country and she chose to remain in Japan to await his return. She bought many valuables with all the money she had saved and sent them on with my brother, believing that she too would soon be going to Korea. But because she believed that were I to marry Iwao, I would be mistreated by his Japanese family, she felt that I should not be left alone to take this dangerous chance. She betrayed me and disclosed my secret to Nam Hak, an action that changed my life 180 degrees.

Striking me, he said, "You are my responsibility since our father is gone. I can't leave you alone in Japan." His words seemed like those of a responsible man, but he never at any time took care of me and my family; never, ever! I wanted to escape just as the boat was leaving, but I later came to believe that we have a fate that cannot be changed by one's own power.

I don't know if it was deliberate, but my mother drank ethyl alcohol before boarding the ship. It might have been her way of resisting, although people did drink diluted ethyl alcohol in the absence of a quality alcoholic beverage. She opposed our return to Korea, but had depended on my brother completely after my father's death. She was not in a position to express her own opinion and it's my belief that she felt suicide to be her only choice. Nam Hak and his wife insisted, however, that we all go on with his plan, that the schedule could not be changed and that he had spent all he had to charter the boat. He forced our mother aboard although she remained unconscious. I, too, felt I had no choice. I could not leave my mother on the ship in that condition and I boarded very reluctantly. Musing on how quickly I could return to Japan, I didn't write to Iwao. How could I have known then that my first love ended right there at the quay.

Once Nam Hak had left with all her goods, Nam Bong and her three children lived in unimaginable poverty. The Japanese government did not provide pensions to the families of Korean soldiers who had been drafted; so, many, many families were not spared the starvation that was rampant at the war's end. Her debts were so great that she was forced to remain in Japan, where she died just a few years ago. Eventually, her husband was sent back to Korea and obtained my sister's belongings, but he was forbidden to travel to see his family at that time. We still don't know his whereabouts to this day.

My mother regained consciousness on board and we returned to our house on Cheju Island, which I saw for the first time. It was the house and farmland my parents had bought little by little as they struggled financially. Now, all of it belonged to my brother, although my mother owned it legally and should have had rights to everything. But because she was old and uneducated, she was deprived of her property. My sister-in-law's family lived next door and it was her family that had looked after our house and the mulberry field behind it. A mulberry field was valuable back then. Shortly after we settled in, Nam Hak and his wife began talking of removing us from the house. She was a beautiful, outspoken, and hard-working woman. It was she who had decided to return to Korea because she knew the value of her family's resources, and it was she who refused my mother permission to use the mulberry field.

My mother, however, was able to rent a small two-room house from a relative, the house being detached from the main living quarters. She had wanted to use the mulberry field to prepare for my marriage sometime in the future. I had no immediate plan to marry, but I was already twenty years old. Nevertheless, not only did Nam Hak and his wife reject my mother's request, they also refused to provide her with food! As a result, she was forced to help other neighbors cultivate their fields and was paid in rice and potatoes. I cannot imagine her frustration and anguish, but I was too busy thinking about how to return to Japan, rather than her despair.

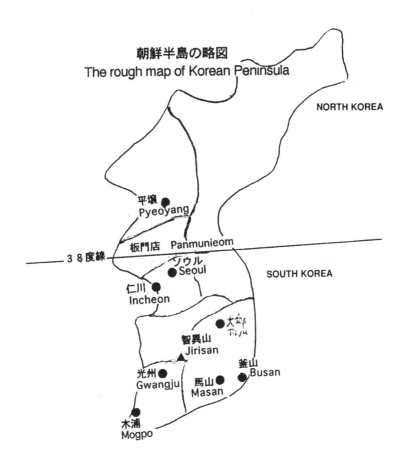

朝鮮半島の略図
The rough map of Korean Peninsula

NORTH KOREA

平壌●
Pyeoyang

板門店 Panmunieom
３８度線

ソウル
●Seoul

SOUTH KOREA

仁川●
Incheon

大邱
Taigu

智異山
▲Jirisan

光州●
Gwangju

馬山●
Masan

釜山●
Busan

木浦●
Mogpo

済州
●Jeju
Jeju do

JEJU ISLAND

▲漢拏山
Hanrasn

西帰浦
●Seogwipo

Two
Korea

Cheju Island

After I had been there some time, I learned the extent of the Island's underdevelopment when contrasted with mainland Korea. Cheju is the largest island off the Korean peninsula, and it is noted for its pleasant spring-like weather throughout the year. At the south end of the island is a town called Seogipo, famous for its waterfall. About three miles away is the small, poor village of Seohori, where my parents bought their house and farmland. This warm-weather island is also known to be very windy, have a stony terrain, and women! It is so windy that the sea is always at high tide and the pumice covering the island is said to be the aftermath of an eruption of a volcano, the Hanrasan, located in mid-island.

Field work was done by the men, but when they came home, they looked after their children or attended village gatherings to play cards and discuss local events. Women not only worked the fields with their men but also did the household labor, sometimes raising silkworms as a part-time job and spinning silk far into the night. The women of Cheju were and are well-known for their energy and diligence. When they had no field work, they would dive into the sea for abalone and seaweed, which they sold. Kitchens could barely be called rudimentary, having neither water systems nor sinks. Most households had two big black iron pans used to boil water and steam potatoes. The cooking heat, called "*ondoru*," was used to warm the room from beneath the floor in winter, although the winters were not at all harsh. In later years electricity was finally brought to Cheju, but our

37

Japanese currency could not be used to pay for it. Instead, we used camellia oil for light after dark.

There are still three large open vents at the top of the Hanrasan, and a local legend tells that three men with the family names Koh, Yang, and Bu were born of the vents. Other surnames on Cheju are derived from the descendants of political criminals in the time of the Lee Kingdom. My surname, Koh, is one of those mentioned in the legend, and I am, therefore, a descendant of the ancient founders. Koh, Yang, and Bu were all related and thus were not supposed to intermarry, even now. Of course, young people these days don't respect the old traditions and ignore them when they decide whom they will marry.

Oddities cropped up from time to time, as when a man in his seventies began a conversation, addressing me in honorific language. I was not sure of the reason, but was told that he was a Sannomu, and Sannomus were obliged to address even Yanban children in those terms. The Sannomu and the Yanban are remnants of the class system in existence during the Lee Kingdom. If one were born into a Sannomu family, holding public office was excluded no matter how capable the individual. One had to live a lifetime as a slave of the Yanban, and their children would have the same fate generation after generation. On the other hand, no matter how stupid, a Yanban could easily become a powerful public official, and use the Sannomu as servants or slaves, as they pleased. This class system faded after the Sannomu left for the mainland, where they educated themselves and found work they merited. Yet this was based on withholding the truth about their backgrounds. Now, I think I should be grateful that I wasn't born into a period of class discrimination, but back then I was too preoccupied with my own life to take notice of it.

One advantage of this island was the absence of thieves. There were no entrance doors on any house, and instead, each house had a log in the entryway. When someone was at home, half the log was put down. Another interesting practice was that most of the households kept pigs in their toilets. "Toilet" is a rather overstated term, because in this context it was actually a stone wall without a roof and an umbrella was needed when it rained. Two logs were placed across the wall and poor people simply squatted to answer a call of nature. The pigs served as waste disposals, eating both leftover food and human excrement. The reality was that poor people didn't have the money to buy even a pig to breed. Wealthy villagers could afford to roof over the stone wall, or sometimes had a modern facility installed, but the majority of villagers were poor and uneducated. If you were so inclined, you might think it convenient to have the pigs clean up leftover food. But for me, answering a call of nature was a real issue and I was so frightened of the pigs! The common wisdom was that the meat from pigs raised on human waste was tasty. I don't know the truth of that statement, but I have to admit that the pork we had occasionally was delicious indeed. Perhaps anything would have tasted good to a hungry person.

In fact, the area in which I lived was the most uncivilized in Korea. The idea that I was to live my life there, farming the land, drove me crazy. Today, its year-long spring-like weather has made this once uncivilized island a major tourist attraction, especially for honeymooners. I have been told that Cheju will become an international tourist spot where, in the future, passports will not be required. It is also the only tangerine-producing area in Korea; both my nieces sent their seven children (collectively) to college by cultivating tangerines. I am proud of them They had worked hard.

I used to think that all of Korea had a culture either the same or similar to Cheju Island's, and discovered only later that the Korean mainland manifested a civilized lifestyle not too different from that of Japan. Yet, at the time, my desire to go back to Japan was growing stronger every day and the desire was frustrated because I had no money whatever. Had I been born on Cheju, I would have adopted its traditions and economy, but I had been born and raised in the Japanese culture. I simply could not adapt to this new life. When the weather was nice, I used to walk up the hill and look far away across the sea at the silhouette of Japan. I thought about my sister, Nam Bong, who still lived there with her three-year-old and six-year-old children, wondering how she was, and if she were still waiting for her husband to return. I thought about Japan and my childhood friends, with whom I picked pine leaves and branches. I thought about my life as a student nurse at the hospital, and about Iwao Miyamoto, a man whose hand I had never held and who had written to me of marriage.

Were all those dreams—or was my current life a dream? I wanted wings. I wanted to fly to Japan, and when I saw a ship far away on the ocean, I thought about swimming out to it and asking for help. But I knew it was unrealistic. What then should I do? I had to get away from that medieval village somehow. If I remained, I would marry a farmer and become like those strong Cheju Island women who raise silkworms and give birth to children who would repeat the same existence one generation after the other. I could not stand it! I decided to leave Cheju at least, and take my chances on the Korean mainland. Yet, how impossible was that—considering my financial situation?

Running Away from Home

I had left my belongings in Japan with Nam Bong because I planned to return quickly, so I had no goods to sell for cash nor did Japanese currency have any value. Fortunately, my mother had a few kimonos that she must have brought in preparation for my anticipated marriage. I could sell the kimono cloth as linen or as fabric for covering a comforter, so, secretly, I did sell one of her kimonos—for 2,000 wone. My destination was Kyongsun (now Seoul), the capital of Korea. When I left home, I told my mother that I was visiting an aunt in the north for a week. Actually, I never returned to the village of Seohori except when visiting my mother and Nam Gi from time to time.

My greatest hope was that my nursing license would keep me from starvation. In the meantime, a ferry in northern Cheju took me to Mogpo, the closest city on the Korean mainland, where a childhood friend of Nam Bong had her home. Money was in short supply and I had only 1,200 wone left after buying the ferry and bus tickets. Moreover, I didn't speak Korean, although I could understand a bit of the Cheju dialect. It wasn't until I boarded the ferry that I realized how terribly different it was from the Korean spoken on the mainland. As the ferry pulled away from the dock, I looked back at the island and thought about my mother and younger sister, concerned about their future and my own. It was very windy, and the ferry became so unstable in the high tide that I developed motion sickness. Finally, we arrived at Mogpo. Those who disembarked were all walking in the same direction. I

41

had no idea of where they were going, but I followed them anyway. Their destination, I was relieved to learn, was the train station.

A Language Barrier

I resolved to speak Japanese in case of emergency, as Koreans had spoken it before the war's end. But I was mistaken: by the time I arrived in Mogpo, Japanese had been prohibited by the Korean government. I was able to read only some of the Chinese characters on the posters at the station, but not Hanguru, Korean script. I was completely lost and missed the train to Kyongsun by a moment. Hearing someone speaking the Cheju dialect, I discovered that the next train was scheduled for 7:00 A.M. the next day. If I stayed at a hotel, I would not have had enough cash for the train ticket. I just didn't have the money! I wanted to cry, but I decided instead to look for my sister's wealthy friend, whom I had never met. Again, language itself was a problem—I couldn't even ask directions, although I had her written address, so I needed to check the tag on each house I passed. Many hours later, I found the house, but Nam Bong's friend was away: she was in Japan. Her aunt, a woman in her fifties, and the housemaid explained the situation in the Cheju Island dialect. Apparently, wealthy people frequently vacationed in Japan and traveled via black market boat. At last, sitting on the floor, I began sobbing, and, in Japanese, tried to explain my own situation. They replied that they would ask their family-practice physician whether he could hire me as a nurse so that I wouldn't have to go to Kyongsun and they encouraged me by insisting that I *would* learn Korean. In Korea those days, Chinese characters were still written and read, so I took advantage of knowing those used by the Japanese, and tried to learn Korean whenever I had the time. About six months later, I was able to speak a little Korean, although I could hear my heart pounding when I did so. Luckily, I got the live-in nursing position at the doctor's small practice very quickly. My sleeping area was a small space under the stairway, but don't get me wrong. I was not complaining. This was like running into Buddha in hell!

The doctor suggested I transfer my Japanese license to a Korean one at the local government office. It was a simple process, in fact, and I obtained a license to practice nursing in Korea without any trouble. Looking back, I would have had a completely different life had I gone on to Kyongsun My job, however, was not exactly nursing, but more that of a maid. Yet, I did administer venous injections, which I hadn't done in Japan, and I did have many other opportunities there in Mogpo. One day, I felt a chill. I took my temperature and it was 41 degrees C. Aspirin was able to keep my temperature in check, but I felt chilled again later that afternoon. This went on for about a week until the doctor finally diagnosed it as malaria. I was prescribed Quinine and recovered, but this incident convinced me to look for a post at a large hospital. The biggest one near Mogpo was the Kuangju State Hospital. I wrote a resume and sent it to the director of nursing, not thinking I would be hired, but I got the position.

Kuangju Medical University Hospital

The dormitory I lived in at Kuangju Hospital was the same type as the one in the nursing schools of Japan: a small tatami room (the size of 4 ½ tatami mattresses), which four nurses shared, as we worked different shifts and barely saw one another. Meals served in the dorm cafeteria were always a mixture of rice and soy beans in order to conserve the rice. For breakfast, a soup was served, just like the one in Japan, but kimchi (fermented cabbage) replaced the Japanese radish pickles. At lunch, we ate rice and two sheets of dried seaweed per person, with a bottle of soy sauce on the table as a condiment. Usually, we wrapped the rice with the seaweed and kimchi was always a side dish. The war was over, but Japan and Korea were both still poor.

Nurses were permitted to come and go freely, and many would go home to bring kimchi and other foods back to the dorm. My background was different from that of the others and language was an issue as well, so I was always isolated and never shared in the extra food or camaraderie. I did my best to learn Korean, but I couldn't make much progress. My pronunciation was bad and the other nurses avoided speaking to me: every time I tried to speak, my pronunciation was ridiculed—it was the object of their amusement. It was so difficult to learn the language, and though I mentally practiced what I wanted to say, the thought process was very slow and, in fact, I was too slow to hold a conversation. In addition, I was raised in the Japanese culture of self-efface-ment, an important and beautiful tradition. Within that tradi-tion, I was an outgoing person; now, however, it only added

45

to my sense of utter exclusion. It was natural that I would develop feelings of inferiority.

Kuangju medical school hospital in Korea working as a nurse in 1949

More action than words! I resolved to work extra hard as I had when I made so good an impression at the military hospital. When on the night shift, I checked each room in the middle of my shift, and did the same before the shift changed, giving my patients more help and support. I had learned a few Korean phrases, and I made it a point of asking, *"Pyorugo oppusuminka?"* (Is everything all right?) I practiced the phrase many times so as not to make mistakes when I actually spoke. Then I knocked on the door, smiled, and repeated it, *"Anyang haseyo. Pyorugo oppusuminka?"* (Good morning. Is everything O.K.?). An older woman who was attending a

46

patient looked at me in confusion and replied, *"Aniyo pyor-uck oppusoyo."* (No, we don't have fleas here!) Of course, we were speaking at cross-purposes, but another TB patient in the room (a school teacher) understood what I meant, told me that everything was fine, and thanked me for stopping by. I was pleased. My language skills may have been poor, but it was worth trying.

Soon afterward, the State Hospital became the Kuangju Medical University Hospital, and the nursing school was upgraded as well. I was asked to be mistress of ceremonies at the welcome party for first-year nursing students. To this day, I don't know why I, who barely spoke their language, was assigned the role. Perhaps they thought my Korean, with its Japanese accent, was funny. Or, was it because of my humorous personality? I did well, however, and everyone enjoyed my dance, set to the Japanese folk song, *"Kojo no Tsuki"* ("Moon above an Old Castle"). The result of my efforts was an invitation to a gorgeous dinner at the home of the president of the hospital, a gynecologist/obstetrician. It was one of the incidents that gradually persuaded me to remain in Korea instead of returning to Japan, and eventually I was encouraged as my use of Korean improved, easing my ability to communicate with both patients and staff. At the time, the Dermatology/Urology Department where I worked had few patients, so I considered studying something new in my spare time. I discovered then that some nurses in OB (obstetrics) were studying for a midwife exam scheduled for the following fall. I decided to take the challenge of this exam.

A Licensed Midwife

In those days, the Kuangju didn't have a department for midwifery where students could train, so we had to study on our own to qualify for a license. It was about three years since I had left Japan for Korea, and I was able to read and write the Korean language at last. But, to my advantage, medical terminology was written mainly with Chinese characters, which use the same characters in Japanese, and I was accustomed to reading those terms in Japanese. When it was slow during my shift in dermatology/urology, I studied in the exam room. I asked help from a nurse in OB and she allowed me to attend childbirths in my free time. Luckily, a doctor was kind enough to tutor me if he wasn't busy. "Hands-on" education was so different from the textbook learning with which I was struggling. For example, I was edgy, but I examined the cervix of a pregnant woman with my finger and was able to discern that it was three fingers dilated, confirming the fact to the doctor who had just examined her. Whether he questioned me to assist the learning process or simply to ascertain my competency, his responses were a saving grace. It was like walking in the dark at first; yet, as I became accustomed to the situations, I began hoping to deliver a baby by myself, and one day I did it! The doctor stood beside me, looking on. "Miss Koh, you did great!" he said. I was so proud of myself and so excited that I couldn't sleep that night. I thought, "Oh, it's easy." However, I was not always able to do it by myself—I needed the doctor's help the next few times and he disciplined me each time, insisting that a midwife needed more patience. I began to fear childbirth and lost confidence.

The day of the exam finally arrived; it was divided into two parts, written and practical. I did well on the written test because the medical terms were principally in Chinese characters (Japanese vocabulary), although I had a hard time with the practical. I was very nervous and found it difficult to explain in Korean. An overweight examiner official reacted with sarcasm when I told her that I was not fluent in Korean. "Are you going to speak English, then?" she responded. The woman later was appointed chairperson of the Korean Midwife Association and eventually I was appointed a manager. At the time of the exam, however, I never thought I would be working with her in the future.

I somehow passed the exam, but I don't recall being happy or excited, perhaps because I had no one with whom to share the good news. When I wrote my mother, she must have believed that the midwife license would bring me a decent income and she soon came to Kuangju to live with me. She was mistaken: my salary was very little and she was not permitted to stay at the dorm, I had to ask her to find a cheap house outside Kuangju City and support herself. My mother was nevertheless adamant in her desire to remain, replying that it was better to do that than return to Cheju Island. To worsen the situation, Nam Gi came to live with my mother. None of us had any savings and I could find consolation only in the old saying that "If you have no teeth, your gums will replace them." I hoped that we would find something else if we had no money. Another Japanese adage tells us, however, that "When you choose to take care of your parents, they are no longer around." Looking back, I regret not looking after my mother. I wish I had done more for her, and when I think of her now, I can't stop crying.

The Korean War Intervenes

While writing this book, I came across another by chance, *Korea: The Untold Story of the War*, by Joseph C. Goulden, published in 1982. It concerned a government secret of the Korean War that could be disclosed only after the statute of limitations had been reached. I read the Korean version published in June 2002, translated by Byong Cho Kim, M.D. I had never known these facts before. I would suggest you read the book if you want to know more, but let me explain it briefly. When the treaty of friendship between Japan and Russia was signed in 1896, Japan, Russia, and China were battling over the rights to the Korean Peninsula, at that time in the period of the Lee Kingdom. The term "north latitude 38 degrees" appeared in the lexicon around that time. Goulden's book explained that Japan and Russia had signed a secret agreement allowing Russia political and economic rights in the northern section of the Peninsula, and Japan the same rights in the southern area. Japan then invaded Seoul and destroyed the Lee Kingdom, while Russia ruled in the north. Those who were opposed defected to Manchuria or southern Korea.

Theodore Roosevelt, president of the United States, approved Japan's right to Manchuria and Korea on condition that Japan did not invade the Philippines. Thus, regardless of the 1882 friendship treaty already existing between the United States and Korea, Korea was subjugated by Japan, an unimaginable shock to the Korean population. Economic and political power were no longer in the hands of Koreans; we were no longer an autonomous nation. These unfortunate conditions have become a part of our heritage in folk song and tales.

Under foreign rule, Korean families were driven apart from one another. Those who remained in the North suffered with hunger and exposure to many freezing days and nights. Now, the issue of North and South Korea is still terrifying not only to Koreans, but to peoples the world over. There are countless sad stories arising from this horrific history, but I realized that my experiences were among the worst of these victims. If General MacArthur had not arrived at Inchon at the last minutes of September 15, 1950, my home in southern Korea would have been burned along with the others, and starvation would have been as severe as in the North. My children and I would not enjoy the happiness we now enjoy had it not been for him. "A shrimp is crushed in a battle of the whales"; this old adage says it all.

On June 25, 1950, Sunday before dawn, the North Korean army, supported by Russia and her weapons, attacked South Korea.[2] This was the infamous incident of June 25th. The Korean Peninsula was divided into two political regions, communism in the North, and a republic in the South: war broke out. Kuangju was still quiet, but because it was close to the communist base at Mt. Chili, there were many communists in Kuangju. Police searches were rigorous and particularly focused on the elite medical students or nurses, who were sometimes brought to police headquarters, not once, but several times. They were detained at least four to five days in prison and badly beaten. I heard a rumor that elites who simply met or joined reading or friendship groups to pursue their cultural interests, such as literature, were summoned by the police. They and some medical students never returned from their interrogations. Most of the medical staff

---

[2] Goulden, Joseph C., *Korea: The Untold Story of the War.*

were called before the police, one by one. I was language-handicapped and had not been recruited by any groups. Perhaps that was the reason the police never questioned me.

A rumor soon spread that the North was coming down to the South rapidly. Hospitals had no choice but to send all the patients home or evacuate them. I had saved 240 wone by then, and I gave eighty wone each to my mother and Nam Gi, cautioning them to return to Cheju Island quickly. I went back to the hospital. I had no home to go to, so I got together with other nurses who were in the same circumstances as I, and we resolved to remain there as long as possible before escaping as a group. I left eighty wone and my everyday goods with a friend and was still wearing a white uniform and cap, nursing incoming wounded at the hospital till the end. At some point, I looked around and noticed that the doctor, our hospital president, and I were the only ones there. It was then that a soldier with an arm MP band aimed his rifle at me and said, "The chief was shot. He's in a jeep and you must treat him *NOW*." I tore outside, where the street was filled with people fleeing. Did they know their destination? I don't know. Some carried their possessions on their heads, walking at a fast pace. Fathers pulled rickshaws with children and belongings piled on. Mothers followed, pushing the clumsy vehicle from behind. Young people fled without belongings of any kind.

I followed the doctor, climbing onto the roofless jeep with our medicine case. The officer had been shot in the leg and was sitting in the back seat with the leg propped up. Around him were other soldiers. As soon as we began treating him, the driver turned on the ignition, saying that they had no time. The jeep couldn't move fast, though, because the huge crowds were blocking the streets. The doctor and I were surprised, but we had no choice except to go along with the soldiers. As I had left my 80 wone behind, I was completely penniless, and frightened of what might happen the next moment. The Southern army must have been very shaken to learn that the North was descending upon them. I was told later that most soldiers wearing MP arm bands were, in fact, police officers, and because the police were so brutal in their search for communists, the North would kill them on the spot when they were found. The MP (military police) arm band was being used to camouflage the police officers' identities.

We treated the officer's wound and were sitting in the passenger's front seat of the jeep, watching the people running down the streets, thinking that my luck was better than theirs, when I felt a sharp pain in my right shoulder. I thought that the soldiers in the back seat struck me, but I soon became light-headed and leaned forward to the doctor. I heard the soldiers shout, "The nurse has been shot!" I finally realized that I had, indeed, been wounded. Rather than the pain of a blow to my shoulder, I felt a heavy weight on it. It was, however, only a piercing bullet wound. The bullet entered from above my right shoulder blade and exited again just two centimeters below my collarbone. If it had entered a bit lower, the bullet would have hit my lung, and had it entered a bit higher, the collarbone would have seen crushed. It's awful to be shot, but how lucky that I had been shot where I had been. I don't know who pulled the trigger, but I think it was a mistake that occurred because a soldier in the back had neglected to set his safety clip. Seconds later, someone with the arm band of a medical orderly showed up from nowhere and climbed into the jeep. He cut my uniform around the wound with surgical scissors, treated it quickly, applied gauze, and bandaged it with a towel. He administered a penicillin injection and gave me a warm drink, and then he left without ever telling me his name. I didn't even have the opportunity to look at his face. I always regret that I didn't thank him, although more than fifty years have passed.

We arrived in a town called Masan in Kyongsun Num Do, and the soldiers dropped us off at a small medical clinic. The doctor, my traveling companion, overheard that the army hospital was moving from Kuangju to Masan, and left me there, saying he would be in contact. I was alone at the clinic, and a stranger. I had not a cent nor an extra fragment of cloth to sell, so I just sat there, waiting to hear from him. I wondered about my mother's and sister's well-being, and about what I would need to do to survive, but I couldn't think of an answer.

Long hours passed and it was already dark. The clinic staff seemed annoyed that I was still there, and my repetitive thought was whether he would ever contact me again. When I had just about given up, rescue arrived. The doctor arranged to transfer me to the army hospital for treatment, and I would be able to continue my nursing there after recovery. That was, again, a "Buddha in hell" situation. I was so appreciative of the doctor for his great kindness.

Two weeks passed before I fully recovered from the wound. Meanwhile, my white uniform was replaced with military olive-drab, although I didn't have a wone, and so could not buy personal items. I guess my plight aroused sympathy among the staff, because the kitchen's chef generously offered me some cash to buy toiletries. Again, I felt I had been saved, and I thought of the truth in another old proverb, "There is no demon where you want to go." I was happy enough until the chef came to me one day with a different offer: "I found you a small room in the city," he said. "You can move out of the hospital and live there. I will pay your expenses so you won't have to worry about anything." Then I realized why he was so kind to me, and I was very disappointed. He must have been selling military commodities on the black market to earn the money for keeping a mistress in the city. The mistress in this case was to be me! I knew from hospital chatter that he had a wife and children at home and I began considering what could occur if he were discovered. It would not be long before the military discovered his theft and he would be ousted. Then he would come to me, begging for help, and I would be blamed for everything he had done. I felt like vomiting! All of a sudden, I really hated this man. Needless to say, I rejected his proposition, and sometime afterward, the hospital was paying for my work—a small amount to be sure—but something.

The war continued. More and more casualties were brought in every day. Some lost their eyes, others, their legs. Some were covered with blood, others suffered from tetanus and were arched over due to horrible muscular contractions. So many wounded were laid on the hallway floors, waiting for death. It was a picture of hell. But I had to work and make my way around their bodies no matter how terrible it was. With the ever-nearing Northern army, the hospital was ordered to relocate to the southern end of the Korean Peninsula, Pusan. We had gone as far as was possible. There was no place for us to go anymore. Pusan was packed with people who had escaped from North Korea and the coffee shops were filled to capacity with job-seekers and those trying to sell something. It was a bizarre setting: a grotesque sort of festival. Their scanty meals were rice and kimchi, which many shared with the starving, who didn't even own a bowl from which to eat. Their bits of rice tasted remarkably wonderful to the hungry.

Nurses were being asked to update our resumes and apply for the rank of second lieutenant in the Southern army. I, too, applied, but a student nurse was promoted instead of me by mistake. I was asked to apply again, although a number of patients indicated that, as a woman, I would have no need of the rank. I regret to say that I actually took their advice, although it must have been fated that I would. Still, I had to leave the hospital immediately and endured a great deal of hardship as a consequence. I wonder, occasionally, how different life would have been had I been appointed second lieutenant. On the other hand, I may not have met my wonderful husband, Larry, in the distant future.

In Custody

At the moment, I lived with Nam Bong's friend in Pusan, but it was not easy to find a job in that overpopulated city. One day, I ran into another nurse who hadn't been promoted either and she mentioned having found a post at the POW (prisoner of war) hospital. I applied to the hospital at once, and, fortunately, I was hired.

The "hospital" was a temporary series of tents in an open field operated by the Americans, and treated North Korean soldiers, including women, who had been caught in the South. All the nurses were Americans. Most of the newly hired Korean nurses did not speak English, and I was not an exception. I had *never* seen Westerners before and was intrigued by their variety: blonde, blue-eyed, Black, and White. I'm embarrassed now to think of my ignorance! Imagine, I didn't understand the reason towels didn't become discolored after use by a Black nurse! Communication with the American staff had to be done through translation by some nurses who could speak both Korean and English.

I recall a day when the head nurse gave me a direct order in English because the translator couldn't be found; I didn't understand a word she said, which was, I later learned, "Wash the face of that patient whose arm was amputated." Realizing that I did not understand her, she gestured to me with her arms: she pointed her arm and said, "Sayonara," then acted out washing her own face, and saying, "Wash! Wash!" At last, I understood. I thought it funny that she had said good-bye to her arm. Yet, it was that humorous gesture that helped me fathom what she wanted to say.

57

Although they were POWs, we spoke the same Korean language and I sympathized with their situations. Nevertheless, we were not supposed to speak with them about anything personal. This hospital was well-supplied with penicillin and other medical necessities shipped from the States. A few patients who were only slightly injured pretended to swallow their medications, but actually kept them aside. They then asked those of us who commuted to and from the city to sell the medications for cash and buy rice cakes or different foods, which they shared with the others. This, too, was an open secret that no one revealed.

One morning after I had been working there five or six months, police officers came in and searched all the personal belongings of the nurses who commuted. Obviously, someone had reported the transactions to the hospital management or police. Nurses who had only food were released, but I had a notebook and a pencil in addition to the rice cakes. That was unfortunate. They suspected that the notebook and pencil were communication tools, and I was taken into custody for espionage activities. Now, with my personality being what it was, I could *never* have been a spy, and it was absurd that I was mistaken for one. In the United States, in 2005, I can laugh at the incident; back then, however, I was very frightened. The police didn't torture me, but they treated me like a criminal and I had to put up with severe humiliation. I did not comprehend any reason I had to submit to this harassment, and railed at my difficult life. I felt I did not want to live anymore.

I was fed barley and radish leaves, along with the sand that hadn't been washed from them. Still, I always longed for the next meal! Strangely (to me in my naivete), the police ordered me to report the conversations of my cell-mates. Thus, instead of being subjected to torture, I was now commanded to be a police spy! In fact, I really didn't hear a thing and don't remember ever reporting anything. I was occasionally taken to interview rooms for questioning by the officers, but that was all. Almost a month had passed since my arrest; no one visited me during that time, and I heard that I was to be transferred to prison shortly. Once in prison, I thought, would I ever be released? Jean Valjean, the protagonist of the Hugo novel, *Les Miserables*, came to mind, and a chill crept over me. "What wrong did I do? Do they really think I'm a spy? I did my very best at the hospital." I regretted ever empathizing with the POWs, but it was too late and nothing I could do. At the end of thirty days, however, I was released because the police could not find any proof to support their accusation.

A Refugee in My Own Country

Then what? I lost my job because of the arrest, and I was looking for work all day, everyday. I was always hungry, but so stressed worrying about my future, that hunger seemed unimportant. Nam Bong's friend was so kind and tried to encourage me. But I was a lodger sharing her small room in her house and I didn't want to burden her more than was necessary. I made a point of not being at home at meal times so that she wouldn't have another mouth to feed. I even lied, saying my friends were taking me out to dinner.

In Pusan, a great number of people were starting businesses, but I had no business sense nor any seed money. My only chance for survival was a nursing post, but I was unable to find one and was in despair of ever finding one. At last, I saw a sign reading, "Red Cross Hospital," and without any hope, I applied to the director for a job interview. A man in his fifties came out to meet me. This was Dr. Seo. The director of the hospital was away serving as a military physician during the war. Dr. Seo, a friend of the director and an OB who had been evacuated from Taegu, was now acting director in the director's absence. He hired me without delay because I had both nursing and midwife licenses and experience.

Dr. Seo received his MD from the Hospital of Kyushu Medical University in Japan and we hit it off immediately. In those days, MDs had to be exceptionally bright and I respected him for his efforts to achieve his position. More than anything, I was happy that I no longer had to suffer hunger. I heard once, "When you hit bottom, you can only come up from there." I believe it.

There were about ten rooms in this hospital, all of them filled with refugees from North Korea rather than local patients. Everyone slept on the floor. Compared to those refugees, the staff, two doctors and two nurses, lived in luxury, in separate rooms. Our meals were steamed yellow millet every day, and the doctors always complained. For me, it was a golden meal. One night at around 11 P.M., after the doctors had gone to bed, someone pounded on the hospital door and woke me. "Help! Doctor, help!" the voice exclaimed. I went out and saw a middle-aged man standing there, his head covered with blood. He said that he had had a fight and had been struck. He pressed a cloth to his injured head and was assisted by his family. I cleaned the wound and realized it was not very severe, but there were some glass cuts that needed to be stitched. I reported this to the younger doctor, who asked me to see to the patient myself and agreed that I should suture the wounds. He said that he would take responsibility for my work and promptly pulled the blankets over his head.

I told the injured man that the doctor was out and that I would look after him. Borrowing a doctor's gown, and pretending to be calm, I cut the patient's hair around the injuries and applied a disinfectant solution followed by alcohol. Having observed suturing at the army hospital, I was able to attend to the patient on my own. At the conclusion of the procedure, I administered penicillin. Often in such cases, though, the patient tends to feel better if more medications are used, so I also injected him intravenously with 20cc calcium and glucose. This injection suffuses the body with internal warmth and another, Vitamin B, enhances the patient's sense of well-being. I sent him home with the admonition to return the next day to see a doctor. His family was so pleased.

While I was treating the man, the mother of the director was at the hospital. She wanted to bill them for the basic procedure and for the additional medications, which raised the cost. (Her calculations were actually lower than the correct charges.) The family was nevertheless so pleased with both the care and the cost, they included a tip for me. This also pleased the director's mother and provided extra income for the hospital. Everyone talked about the incident the following day and I was served white rice at the meal instead of yellow millet. We all laughed at what a calculating woman the director's mother was. She was willing to feed me better food only because I had earned a bit of money for the hospital, a recollection that stays with me yet.

About that time, a cease-fire was declared between the North and South. No one was certain how long it would last, but many businesses continued to be opened. In Pusan, anything could be bought and sold and people made large amounts of money. We, the doctors and nurses, whose nature isn't business-oriented, simply envied the success stories. Somehow, I heard that my mother was looking for me then in Kuangju. I had worried about her since she left, but simultaneously was apprehensive at being made aware of just how hard her life had been. I decided to take a week off and visit her. When I asked Dr. Seo's permission, I was surprised by his reply. He said, "If you're going to Kuangju, do you want to conduct some business? Because, if you do, I could invest a little money. I've heard that many people are bringing rice from farms in the countryside and selling it in the city. As a result, the cost of rice has dropped, so we should avoid dealing in rice, but there should be something else we can do. If you agree, we would split the profits." He gave me 100,000 wone, his entire savings. Earning the amount I did, I would have had to work more than a year to earn that kind of money. In any event, I asked him how he could entrust it to me without a guarantee that I would return. Dr. Seo replied, "You don't have the courage to steal the money. If you do not return, there is no one in the world I will ever trust." He probably expected that, in general, people would not be dishonest when they are believed to be so. I was flattered and pleased that he had such faith and confidence in me. Having this amount of cash was a first for me, so I wrapped it in a cloth and tied it around my waist.

I saw my mother, who was doing well, and the friends with whom I had worked at the hospital, but I couldn't find anything for investment. I walked the city every day, looking for something interesting, although I had no business sense and no idea of how to begin. The day before my scheduled return to Pusan, I recognized a man on the street who had worked in the boiler room at the Kuangju Medical University Hospital before the war. We greeted one another, glad that we had both survived the war. He mentioned that he had a retail shop, selling sugar and flour. I talked about having trouble finding a business in which to invest. Of course, he suggested that I buy his flour, and I decided to take his offer rather than return home empty-handed. The retailer saw to everything, from reserving space on a ship, to loading eight straw bags containing the flour. I just watched, doing nothing. The journey to Pusan by sea took two days. During that time, I became seasick and could not eat at all. When we docked, I looked really ill. In the early morning of the third day, owners of cargo were allowed to disembark, but had to wait until 11:00 A.M. to retrieve all their goods. So I took a small flour sample to show to Dr. Seo and went on to the hospital.

Although I had been away two days later than my scheduled return, Dr. Seo welcomed me and took me out to a delicious breakfast. I was concerned about selling the quantity of flour I'd brought, but felt better than I would have had I needed to return all the cash. During our meal, Dr. Seo suggested bringing the flour sample to a local bakery since that was their essential ingredient, of course. We found the largest bakery and showed my sample. To our surprise, the bakers offered to buy the flour for 240,000 wone at once. Dr. Seo and I looked at each other, but he "kept his cool" and answered "OK," calmly. We were *so* excited. In exchange for receipt of eight sacks of flour, Dr. Seo was given his 240,000 wone, which he shared with me as he promised. He was happy and I had a windfall of 70,000 wone. I liked this business! I didn't have to do anything other than show a sample and receive money. I'd never had 70,000 wone in my life and couldn't believe it was real.

Everyone at the hospital was talking about the transaction and many suggested that I do the same with their money. Two hundred-fifty wone were gathered (including my 70,000), and although I wanted to earn more, I was very anxious about the seasickness I would have to endure. I tried to think of other ways to earn a profit and I resolved to buy wheat and have it ground into flour. It took more time than simply buying the flour, but after ten days, I was able to return to Pusan with twenty-five sacks of flour. Naturally, I was sick on the return journey, but I was also exhilarated thinking about the larger profit I was about to make. However, in those ten days, the situation in Pusan was changing dramatically. The United States was donating high-quality flour to feed the refugees and we couldn't sell our flour in Pusan at all. In addition, Dr. Seo was ready to leave for his own Ob-Gyn clinic in Taegu and he was awaiting my return. I came back just as he was about to do so.

I hadn't known that he had closed his clinic because he was suffering from lung disease. He had come to Pusan to recruit a specialist from North Korea because he needed a partner in order to reopen the clinic. He finally met Dr. Lee, who had been a professor at the Medical University of Pyongyang, capitol of North Korea. Dr. Lee agreed to join Dr. Seo's practice and both were on their way to Taegu and I was asked to come along and work for them. We no longer gave any thought to the flour I'd brought back. (Back then, I was too young and inexperienced to raise the issue of payment; and as Dr. Seo didn't mention my 70,000 wone, I tried to convince myself that I'd never had money to begin with, and thus should forget the entire incident. Only now I realize I should have given the 70,000 wone to my mother.) In any event, I rode on the truck Dr. Seo rented and left for Taegu with them.

The OB/Gyn Clinic at Taegu

I was happy to be working in my profession again. The Taron OB/Gyn clinic was once well-known before its closure, but after several years, people had forgotten it. All the equipment still remained; nothing was needed to prepare for the reopening and Dr. Seo's wife must have cleaned the clinic, anticipating her husband's return. It was understandable that we did not have even one patient the first few days, because the hospital had been reopened without an announcement. I suggested placing an advertisement before the opening, but Dr. Seo felt it was inappropriate for the practice of medicine, something that only an incompetent doctor would do. I thought him a stubborn man, but at the same time, admired his pride and confidence. I sometimes think of him when I see advertisements placed by doctors and hospitals these days. Would he believe that those who advertised are incompetents? Dr. Seo developed liver disease and died about five or six years later.

Our first patient was a Kisen (Korea's word for Geisha), an old patient from Dr. Seo's early practice. She was delighted at his return and referred a number of friends to us. It was rewarding to watch our patient population increasing day by day. I was given a place to live in the hospital and food as well. If I helped at deliveries in the home of a patient, the fee became my personal income; if it were in the clinic, it would be the hospital's income. Today, I would have demanded at least my share of the 70,000 wone for the flour and a basic salary, but back then, I was more than happy to have a stable position with food and shelter.

While at the clinic, I heard that placenta hormone was popular in Japan for its benefit to women's bodies and Dr. Seo experimented on the grafting of the umbilical cord. I volunteered to be a guinea pig. First, he severed a three centimeters section of a baby's umbilical cord and placed it in the disinfectant solution, Chloramines. We changed the emulsion everyday and the thick whitish solute gradually thinned over a one-week period, the cord becoming a bright, virginal white. He removed the cord, opened and flattened it, and cut it into one-centimeter pieces. He then grafted this behind my armpit. I was twenty-five years old at that time, still too young to need extra hormone from an external source, and I don't know how this grafting was of benefit. Certainly, there were no side effects, and after about six months, the graft was absorbed into my skin. However, the effect seemed much more apparent on older women. After Dr. Seo repeated the procedure on a woman in her fifties undergoing meno-pause, she told us that she no longer experienced knee pain when walking up and down stairs. Another woman, whose extremities were ultra sensitive to cold, reported that her symptoms were gone following the umbilical graft.

I would now like to share three rare cases that remain in my memory.

Case A

A woman in her thirties was about to give birth to her first child. She came into the clinic every week for an exam after she reached thirty-seven weeks of pregnancy. At the exam in her fortieth week, her cervix was already dilated seven centimeters, but she was not experiencing labor con-tractions. It was the pregnancy she and her family had long awaited, and they were concerned that she might not be able to recognize the signs of birth at all. She was hoping to deliver at home, so I sent her back, telling her to let me know as soon as labor began.

I waited, but did not hear anything for one week. I was disappointed, supposing that she had either given birth on her own or had another midwife help her. In her forty-first week, however, she walked into the clinic by herself, still pregnant and smiling. The doctors were also surprised, but the baby's heartbeat was normal, and I reported to Dr. Seo that her cervix was completely effaced. "Ms. Koh," he responded, "I think it better that you take her home immediately and prepare for labor." I took up my labor kit and brought her home.

When I instructed her family to boil water and have some sheets at hand, she asked me, as if she were merely wondering, "Am I giving birth now?" I told her that she was indeed, and covered the linen with a rubber sheet and a disinfectant cloth. I helped the patient onto the sheet, and I arranged my sterilized instruments after washing my hands in cresol. Although I was nervous, I pretended to be calm. As I conducted an internal exam, my fingers instantly felt the amniotic membrane (which was like an inflated balloon), so I thought it would be an easy delivery. No sooner had I introduced my index and middle fingers and a clamp into the vagina and scratched the membrane just a bit, the woman pushed slightly and the baby was born at once, screaming loudly at the same time. It was a boy. Naturally, the new mother and her family were thrilled at the painless labor.

I checked the umbilical cord, and found it still beating strongly, thus too soon to cut. So, I cleaned the infant's body, first by suctioning the inside of his nose and mouth, and then I wiped his body with a clean cloth. I put one drop of silver nitrate in each of his eyes and gave him a Vitamin K injection. In those days, silver nitrate was used only if the mother could have had a sexually transmitted disease. In fact, she had been infected with gonorrhea by her husband a few years earlier and was treated at the Taron clinic. I administered 0.5 mg Pitocin to accelerate the contraction of her uterus and restore it to normal size. Ascertaining that the pulsing of the umbilical cord had stopped, I clamped the cord with a hemostat, tied it off tightly with disinfected silk thread at three centimeters from the baby and then cut it. I put the infant on a towel so that I could weigh him on the vertical scale. He weighed 3800 grams, a big baby for such an easy labor and delivery. I never, before or since, witnessed a labor as easy. The family was wealthy, appreciated my work, and paid me well. I looked forward to my next visit, when I would bathe the infant and perform a postpartum exam of the mother. I admit that their generous payment encouraged me even more. After all, I was, too, a calculating human being.

Case B

I was awakened by a voice calling out for a doctor. The husband of a pregnant woman told me that his wife's labor had begun three days earlier and the baby had not yet been born, pleading for me to come immediately. I dressed quickly and went to their house. His wife was lying on her back with her knees bent, covered by a thin, dirty comforter in a dark room. Her contractions had stopped and she was unable to straighten her legs. I thought she needed a doctor, not a midwife, but I removed the comforter anyway to examine her. Her naked abdomen was not normal, for it was winding in two, appearing very much like a camel's hump. This was her third birth and because the first two had been so easy, she was incredibly calm. She hadn't needed any help in the delivery of either. I was able to listen to the fetus's heartbeat and it was

69

normal, 144 beats per minute; but the lower wind was the same, and should not have been. I suspected uterine fibrosis (hysteromyoma) and that this was a case for a Caesarean delivery. I asked when she had last urinated and she answered that she had not emptied her bladder in two days. She had been unable to straighten her knees for more than twenty-four hours. Suddenly, I realized that her bladder was the problem, inserting a urethral catheter into it. Well, the urine began flowing like a river. It was nonstop. I had to replace the 500–cc emesis basin four times before her bladder was empty. Instantly, her legs straightened, the membrane broke, and with one push, a big baby boy was born with a lusty scream. I took care of the placenta and cleaned her up (and the floor as well). I applied a previously made white cotton T belt to the vaginal area and put her back on her bed, which lay on the floor. I felt anxious that the mother might bleed excessively after the birth, but during the time it took me to bathe the infant (about thirty minutes), the uterus showed normal contractions and little bleeding. Still, I couldn't leave just yet. The room was heated from below and it should have been warm enough, but the new mother was shivering with cold. Her mother-in-law brought steamed rice and seaweed soup, which a neighbor had prepared, gently encouraging her daughter-in-law to eat it all because her stomach was now empty. The new mother obeyed her, ate everything she was given, and began perspiring. She soon recovered, and when I cleaned her body with a warm towel, she was able to thank me. At last, she fell asleep.

I was amazed by the mother-in-law. Older people do know many good and important remedies, and I learned a great deal from them when I assisted at births in their homes. They taught me nothing technical, but their information was valuable indeed. In this situation, they must have considered me a very fine "doctor" and were pleased. What had happened was simple enough: the uterus had put pressure on the urethra and the bladder was unable to empty itself. This, in turn, interrupted the contractions and blocked the birth canal. So all I did was to merely make it possible for her bladder to function normally. Anyway, I gave the patient a shot of Pitocin and didn't disabuse them of their belief in my abilities. While I spoke with them and was observing the uterine contractions, they served me steamed rice and seaweed soup also. I was glad to have it, and left happily afterward.

In Korea, seaweed soup has traditionally been known to warm the body of new mothers, accelerate milk production, promote blood replacement rich in iron and relieve constipation. So it is customary for her to be fed the soup four or five times daily over a period of one to two weeks. This soup is also the principal meal at birthday celebrations. Since arriving in the United States, I have studied both childbirth and lactation. It's been determined that seaweed soup, which contains many minerals and a lot of iron, is indeed one of the best foods, especially for mothers who raise their babies on breast milk. I would recommend that all new mothers, everywhere, make a point of eating it.

I was pleased that the patient had had a short labor and that the outcome was good. The family gave me a thick envelope with cash inside as I left. I didn't open it there, but discovered later that they paid me 500 wone more than my fee. I felt very warm. I recognized that they were poor and that they had paid me more than was necessary. Midwives' fees largely depend on the generosity of their clients. I have attended wealthy families and some tried to avoid payment. I always believe that those people would pay for their wrongdoing sooner or later. That is my philosophy of life. I might be mistaken. This family, however, was so sincere in their gratitude, and the following seven days of postpartum visits were pleasant to them and to me.

Case C

A thirty-year-old woman came to the clinic because she had been infertile up to that time. She was beautiful, but I thought she lacked femininity. She had been married eight years, never had a menstrual period and was unable to get pregnant. Of course, she was worried. In those days, if a woman could not become pregnant after five years of marriage, she would be called a "stone woman," and be divorced by her husband. Dr. Seo took her medical history and I prepped her for an internal exam. She lay on the examination table, with her legs apart, and I covered her with a sheet. When I saw her genitals, I was shocked, and for a moment I couldn't breathe. Both sides of her vaginal *labia majora* were oddly swollen and appeared strange. I told Dr. Seo that she was ready. A dividing curtain at the patient's abdominal area prevented the doctor and patient from seeing each other's faces. I said nothing, but observed how Dr. Seo's facial expression changed, his eyes widening. Without a word, he placed the index and second fingers of his right hand into the vagina, his left hand on her abdomen, examining both the uterus and the vagina. Then he examined the vulva, and exchanged glances with me. Following the examination, she was sent, fearful and concerned, to await him in his office. I, too, was wondering. He took his chair and said, "I am very sorry, but your uterus is incomplete and you cannot become pregnant." He suggested she take female hormones and gave her a prescription for the tablets. After she left, Dr. Seo explained that she didn't have a uterus, but instead had immature testicles in her *labia majora*. She had both male and female reproductive organs. He had not told her the truth. He had prescribed a lifetime of the hormones from simple consideration for another human being, and I think it was a "lie with good will." What do you think an OB today would do in Dr. Seo's situation?

I have seen many different births and, fortunately, most mothers could offer their babies breast milk. However, before the 1940s, many Koreans lived in extreme poverty and new mothers did not eat sufficiently to produce the necessary breast milk their babies required. So they sometimes appealed to neighbors in the area for a bit of rice, from which they prepared rice gruel and fed it to the infants. They did not know that a neonate's stomach was still too immature to digest any food other than breast milk, so that the infant mortality rate rose pitifully. Thus, it wasn't unusual that a father would avoid registering the baby's birth until the child had survived at least one or two years. Parents were uncertain of whether their baby would live long enough to be registered. My own father also did not register my birth until I was two years old.

Recently, baby formula manufacturers would have us believe that in their first three to four days, newborns must be fed sugar water or bottled (formula) milk to avoid dehydration, which could render a child brain damaged. There is *nothing* that can replace or is better for a neonate than mother's breast milk. Unfortunately there are too many medical professionals who are persuaded by the manufacturer's harangues, and they recommend mothers feed their babies artificial formula, disregarding the benefits of the natural nutrients in breast milk.

Miss L., Communist

The Taron Hospital was the best place to practice as a licensed midwife, but there was a problem. The chief doctors didn't always agree with one another, a normal situation between two professionals. Dr. Seo, the director, had received his MD (and PhD) in Japan, and his partner, Dr. Lee, had been a professor at the Pyongyang Medical University in North Korea. Dr. Lee was a refugee and had been hired by Dr. Seo. Because of this, Dr. Lee felt somewhat inferior to his colleague. Occasionally they became seriously antagonistic over a small incident, and the problem worsened. I didn't know then that I was one of their problems. When he came "aboard," Dr. Lee had hired a nurse with whom he had worked in Pyongyang, so the nurses were divided into two groups.

I was responsible for the financial accounting in addition to my duties as nurse and midwife. At dinner time, I reported all the day's bills before giving the total to Dr. Seo. I imagine that I may have been a bit too precise and must have gotten on Dr. Lee's nerves. One day, he announced that he was leaving. Dr. Seo, who was not well, did not want him to resign. Had it not been for Dr. Lee's assistance, the clinic would not have reopened at all. He did not want to close the clinic again. I offered to quit if that would encourage Dr. Lee to stay on. As a result, the right to manage the clinic was transferred to Dr. Lee, and I was let go. Once again I had nowhere to go, was without money, and felt miserable about my circumstances. I felt I had hit rock bottom—I couldn't drop any further. For a while, a friend I had met in Pusan was kind enough to put me up while I searched for a job. I was disturbed at having to do so, but I needed to depend on someone. One would have to be in the same situation to understand how unhappy I was then. In the interim, I kept liquid morphine on hand for the time when I could no longer face my life, and one day, I drew 10cc of the morphine into the syringe, injecting it in a vein in my left arm, but I didn't have the courage to press the plunger. That's how I failed in my suicide attempt. Most people have no idea what it is like to be alone, unemployed, and indigent.

Finally, however, I found a post at a small surgical hospital. The personnel consisted of only three members: Dr. Kwack, a pharmacist, and a nurse. Today, this hospital in Taegu has become well known, with a staff of hundreds. I could not have had greater appreciation for my nursing license than I did then. Because of it, I was able to find job after job. The wooden building had been a hotel under Japanese government rule. There were more than enough rooms, so that they gave me one of my own. They were also nice enough to place a large sign in front of the hospital announcing that a midwife was on staff. It didn't take long for me to become really busy. Dr. Kwack was a respected doctor with an excellent reputation. The key to his success was his ability to remember each patient's name, even if he had examined the patient just once.

From time to time, my memory dwells on a most unforgettable detective story in which I was involved, when Miss L., a nurse's aide, was hired. This beautiful woman, with pale skin and a nice, quiet smile, had a few years of experience at a hospital managed by the director of Kuangju Medical University. Because of her surgical experience, she was favored by Dr. Kwack and always assigned to assist in the surgical theater. She began accompanying doctors when they visited patients in their homes, even assisting at the removal of an appendix, unthinkable in modern medicine. The surgery was successful and the patient's life was spared, in part because of her abilities. She was the subject of much chatter at the hospital for some time. About then, a male pharmacist was added to the hospital staff, and Miss L. became popular in the pharmacy as well.

She had been born in a small village outside Kuangju, where her mother and brother lived, but she told me they were very poor. Miss L.'s uncle had a dry cleaning store outside Taegu City, and although I saw a man visit her once at the hospital, she didn't seem to know anyone else. Her situation was similar to mine, and I thought we could become good friends. She was a friendly person and shared many private recollections and feelings with me, so I, too, liked her. Nevertheless, I felt badly about myself because everyone talked about her excellent qualities. Soon, however, strange things began to happen.

All I owned back then was my black overcoat, and after saving for two months, I bought myself a black velvet *chima* (skirt) that was trendy—a first, for me. My mother had made me a *chogori* (blouse) from Japanese kimono fabric, and I kept these valuables in my drawer. One day, Miss L. brought back a chemise specially made for a *chima* and said it had been quite inexpensive. One week later, my overcoat was stolen. It was still missing a month later, when a thief broke into another nurse's quarters. I was looking after patients in the examination room at the time, when Miss L. came running in saying, "Miss Koh, your *chogori* was found outside. What happened?" I answered that I knew nothing about it and went to my room with a sense of foreboding. There, I saw that my black velvet *chima* was gone: all my valuables had been stolen. I just sat down and began to cry. Then Miss L. screamed that her 1,000 wone were gone, also, and the small drawer beneath her mirror stood open. A tall fence separated the nurses' rooms from the house next to the hospital. It appeared that a thief climbed over the fence after stealing my *chima* and *chigori,* and Miss L.'s 1,000 wone. In the thief's haste to escape, my *chigori* had been dropped near the fence.

Naturally, the incident created a stir among the staff members, and the doctor responsible for the hospital was concerned about its security and credibility. But for me, a young woman in her twenties, losing all my stylish clothes was a larger issue than the hospital's reputation. I became so distressed and cursed my bad luck. Four or five days afterward while I was seeing to a patient, Miss L. told me that her uncle had a small package sent by her mother in Kuangju. She asked if she could go to her uncle's house to pick it up. I gave her my approval, and said that I was curious about the gift, and would love to see it later.

Miss L. didn't own any dress clothing, so I was happy for her, although she didn't seem excited. She was unable to leave the hospital until evening because we had an onrush of patients immediately after our conversation. She returned in about an hour with the items, the package, of course, already having been opened. She had left the brown wrapping paper at her uncle's house. I asked her what she had received; whatever it was, I was envious that she had someone who could send her a gift. Smiling, she told me that her mother had sent a velvet *chima* and socks. "You can borrow them when you go out." When I saw the *chima*, I thought about my own, which had been stolen. It was depressing. Suddenly, something flashed through my mind: I remembered the chemise Miss L. had bought, even though she didn't have the *chima* itself. It seemed very strange and suspicious to me, and somehow premeditated. The timing was all too perfect, but then again I mused, "Just wait." Her 1,000 wone had also been stolen, and there were footprints on the fence. It was difficult to accept the possibility Miss L. had planned such a scheme: leaving my *chogori* near the fence to deceive me? That was too much! Then again, I had never seen the 1,000 wone in her possession. One suspicion brought on another. Why had she not re-wrapped the gift in its package to bring it back? The paper would have had a mailing address and return address written on it. Besides, her mother was very, very poor, struggling even to feed herself. She could not have sent so expensive an item to her daughter. "No. This is not right," I told myself.

I was certain that Miss L. had stolen my clothing, and began to think of how I might prove her thievery and solve this crime. I needed to be careful because my colleagues might think I was jealous of her popularity. Over and over, I tried to calm myself, but I couldn't control my trembling. While pondering these matters, another friend, who bore no relation to Miss L. or the hospital, visited me there. I brought her to the nurses' quarters and explained every detail of what had occurred. I asked her to go to Miss L.'s uncle's shop, and she was excited and happy to go: she was curious, too. She pretended to be a friend of Miss L.'s from Kuangju, telling him that she had a message from Miss L.'s mother. "She told me that she had sent a package to your address for her daughter two weeks earlier and wanted to be certain it had arrived." He replied that he hadn't received the package yet, "I'm sure it will come soon. Thank you for stopping by."

Breathlessly, my friend reported the conversation to me, which confirmed my theory. At last, I was getting results, but I didn't know what to do with the information. I hesitated to speak to Dr. Kwack the director, who was so fond of Miss L., and I talked with the pharmacists first. Then, on second thought, she might have been perfectly innocent. So, I rented a bicycle and rushed to her uncle's shop to reassure myself before I mentioned the issue to Dr. Kwack. As her uncle saw me, he said, smiling, "A friend of my niece just came here from Kuangju. She mentioned a package, but it hasn't arrived yet. Perhaps it will be here tomorrow."

I was very apprehensive about revealing the situation, but finally, I told him that the "friend" was mine, not Miss L.'s, and I apologized. Then I explained the entire problem. He was visibly shaken and asked me what may seem a silly question,"Did your velvet *chima* have rice sticking to it before?" I replied that it did. Without my being aware, the rice had stuck to it, and I wasn't able to remove the grains perfectly. It was 100% clear that she had stolen my *chima*. Her uncle was still talking to me as I left, and I rode back to the hospital. When I arrived, it was obvious Miss L. had been told of my suspicions by the pharmacists, which I expected. I still remember that her face turned white and her angry look frightened me. She didn't know I had been to see her uncle. "Miss Koh," she said calmly, "I heard you are suspicious of me. But why would I have to go about stealing your clothes in such a devious manner? I'm not that kind of person."

She spoke so ingenuously, I felt as though it were I who had done wrong. I would never win in a verbal confrontation with her. Without taking enough time to think it through, I went to Dr. Kwack. As I anticipated, he rejected my suspicions at first, but eventually, had to admit that her wrongdoing was plausible, as proven by her uncle. However, he called me back later and suggested that she had perhaps lied because her boyfriend may have bought it for her and she had been too shy to say so. I answered that this would not account for the stain on my velvet *chima*. He didn't say another word, but that night asked me, rather than Miss L., to accompany him to the home of a patient. All we spoke about as we walked was Miss L. and the issue. "I can't believe she stole your things, but it seems too clear that she did," he sighed, finally granting that I was right. Nevertheless, the problem was obtaining an admission from her. I resolved to go to the post office the next day to see if records were kept of incoming packages, although I wasn't at all sure that such a tracking system existed. Actually, I thought that I could threaten her with the prospect of going and thus force a confession. When I found Miss L. waiting in our room, she looked calm and, in a soft voice, reiterated that she had never stolen anything and was not the sort of person who would do so. But I knew she was lying. So, in an equally calm voice, I said that the entire problem would be cleared up when I went to the post office to check their records. She answered, "Fine," still "keeping her cool"—cool enough to make me uneasy.

I wasn't certain how long I had slept, but I was awakened before dawn to accompany a doctor on a patient visit. I looked at Miss L.; apparently, she had not slept at all, and burst out, "Miss Koh, I did it. I'm sorry. To tell the truth, I am a communist and I would do anything for my beliefs. Before coming here, I was in a camp deep in Mt. Chili with my communist cell. The man who visited the other day is a member of the group, and when I ran into him on the street, he told me that he had come down from the camp in order to get food supplies. I wanted to help them, so I stole your overcoat and *chima* and sold them. I gave him most of the cash and bought that *chima* with the remainder."

Her confession was unexpected, and Dr. Kwack was even more surprised. Everyone else on staff who were fond of her were similarly surprised and chattered about it continuously. Her activities were a serious political issue and required that we report them to the KCIA (Korean Central Intelligence Agency). The agents came to the hospital immediately and she signed the confession in Dr. Kwack's presence. She was compelled to betray her friend at their next encounter in forty-eight hours somewhere in the city. The hospital was kept under surveillance by undercover KCIA agents round the clock, and anyone entering the hospital was monitored, which annoyed our patients.

On the day of the proposed capture, I was told to go along with the agents as an eyewitness, having seen the man before at the hospital. The agents and I were posted in a nearby watch store where we would have a clear view of the meeting place. I could see many agents posted here and there. At last, Miss L. pointed at a man and said it was he. A short man whom I had *never* seen was instantly arrested and I returned to the hospital. Miss L. did not. She was imprisoned by the KCIA until they ascertained whether the right man had been arrested. The man whom they took into custody as a communist was badly beaten by the agents over several days and then released when his innocence was established. He had nothing to do with communists or communism, only ill luck, and I felt badly for him.

It was about midnight a week after Miss L.'s arrest and I was asleep alone in the bedroom we had once shared. I was awakened by a woman's voice and, opening my eyes, I saw Dr. Kwack's wife. "Miss L. has escaped! The KCIA agents are here searching for her!" I was shocked and asked how and when the escape had taken place. Apparently, in late afternoon, she told the security guards that she needed to use the toilet and there she broke through the glass window, climbing into the adjacent building and fleeing through its entrance. Amazingly, I was there at the time, taking care of a post partum mom and bathing the newborn baby of a lawyer living in that house. The family was in a panic when they discovered that a thief had been in their home and had left by their front door. It was soon settled, however, because nothing had been stolen. I had no idea it was Miss L.!

Again, the KCIA agents took me along in their jeep, this time to locate her uncle's house. It was 1:00 A.M. We couldn't find the address she had given the agents, but they received a call from the hospital and learned that she was hiding there under a floor. I missed her arrest, as I didn't return until after the KCIA left with her. The hospital staff and the patients were still in a state of excitement having witnessed the action. According to the onlookers, she was hidden deep under the floor of the hospital's long corridor. When the agents first entered, it was too dark even for them and they assumed it impossible that a woman would go farther in that gloomy darkness. They came out, but since she wasn't found anywhere else, they decided to search under the floor one more time. One agent, less frightened than the others, crept along with a flashlight and shouted, "I've found you now. I'll shoot if you don't come out." He hadn't found her, but she took the bait. She emerged like a ghost from her hiding place, saying, "I'm coming out," her arms raised behind her head.

I visited Miss L. once in prison to give her some clothes and sanitary pads, but I never saw her again. There is no way of determining the truth of her tale. As I remember, she had had a crush on Dr. Kwack, who was a handsome man, but she had no dress clothes to wear. My guess is that she stole my belongings because she simply wanted to be more attractive to him. But she was caught and she was too embarrassed to admit the real reason. She preferred that he think her a courageous woman who would risk everything for her beliefs. The communist saga was all a lie. I never heard that the man who had visited her was finally arrested. He, too, probably had nothing whatever to do with communism. Miss L. had grown up in Mt. Chili and may have had the ability to do things I could never imagine, but the truth of her life remains a mystery. Afterward, she was the object of discussion for a long time and Dr. Kwack complimented me a bit too much, so that I was somewhat uncomfortable. Anyway, the crime was solved and I had my velvet *chima* back.

Marriage and Midwife Practice

Perhaps because Dr. Kwack's compliments had spread so widely among the patients also, a female patient brought me an offer of marriage. I had neither a home nor a family who supported me. My life had been a hard ride and a lonely one. I didn't think I was a beautiful woman, and was linguistically handicapped, so I always felt myself beneath other people. Naturally, I hadn't many opportunities to meet a man. Without any hope for the future, I had tried to end my life a few times. It was during such a period that this patient told me of the proposal. My intended, Taigin Chung, was a forty-two-year-old man, a boarder staying at her house.

He had graduated from a teacher's college and had taught at the elementary school level, but currently worked for a publisher. Born in the countryside in Northern Kyongsan Do, where his mother still resided, he was the eldest son among three siblings, two boys and a girl. As the eldest, he would be obliged to care for his mother someday, but one could not know how soon that was in the future. He had been married once before, although I never discovered the reason for his divorce. He also had a son, who had been separated from him during the war evacuations, and he did not know if the boy lived or not. I had no complaints about him other than his age, so I decided to meet him; it was my first blind date. I sat behind a screen to hide myself from him; likewise, I could not see his face. "I can't see you if you sit there," he commented. "Come closer and write your name and your registered address here." He handed me a pen and piece of paper—this was more an inquiry than a date! "You have beautiful handwriting," he said, and seemed pleased. I thought back to the day when I was awarded the grand prize in a Japanese calligraphy competition in Hiroshima.

I looked at him and noticed that he wasn't short, had broad shoulders, and made a good impression. He asked if I had any hobbies and whether I enjoyed movies. I answered that I did like movies; as to hobbies, I had been too busy earning a living to indulge in a hobby. Then, he wanted to know how many times I went to see a film in one week's time. I thought, "What? Per week?" I wanted to say that I had *no* time to see that many, but instead, I replied, "Only once in two or three months when a good film is shown." He responded, "I will take you to a film anytime."

He didn't live up to his promise until the end. He took me to a movie once after our blind date, but I was disappointed when I saw him falling asleep in the theater. Several times, Mr. Chung asked me to marry him, but I couldn't decide. I couldn't help but wonder why he was interested in marrying a girl who was neither pretty nor had financial assets; and he still seemed too old for me. Falling asleep in the theater was definitely not an encouraging sign, but since my return from Japan, I had been alone and lonely and without a solid base. I was too lonely and too sad. My only close friend, who was against the marriage, was happily married. I didn't accept her advice as I thought that she hadn't any conception of my loneliness. As I didn't answer yes or no, Mr. Chung interpreted my ambivalence as "yes." And strangely enough I found myself moving toward marriage.

It was then he confessed to having no assets or savings other than his salary from the publishing firm. Earlier, he had told me his family was wealthy, and his assets consisted of a house purchased with the proceeds of his parents' farmland. He used the house to support his former student's political career when the man ran for congress. Now, he was saying that he had nothing. I certainly didn't have the money for a decent wedding ceremony, and told him that I would not marry him if I couldn't have a formal wedding. It was his second marriage and he seemed to think he could start a new family without one. This did not work for me at all. Looking back, I regret having ever married a man who was in poor financial condition, who had originally deceived me, and who was not even willing to provide me with a proper wedding. I wonder if he wished to marry me for *my* income because I was a professional, a nurse-midwife. I wish I could go back in time and undo that marriage, but what was done is done. I just had to accept it as my fate.

Fortunately (or not!), because he was a respected teacher, his former students actually put together our wedding and gave me a watch as a wedding gift. In Korea, it is customary for the bride to buy a set of furniture for her newly married life and bring a wedding gift to the groom's family; but I had been certain to acknowledge my past and current poverty from the beginning of our relationship. So I ignored the custom. We somehow managed the wedding, but hadn't the money to rent a house, or to buy new furniture. Still, I was no longer alone and that made me feel better.

We found a small rental room without a kitchen in a big house just next door to the Taron OB/Gyn clinic where I used to work. This room used to be a guest room in the past. Furniture? He brought just a desk, chest, and a set of bedding of his own. There was no kitchen to do the cooking. I had to use a little portable gas stove. We picked up an apple crate on the street and used it for a kitchen cabinet to display a few rice bowls. I had to get buckets of water from the main building where the landlord lived. Waste water was discarded into the drain outside. Though we were poor, it remains a happy memory because I had been poor for three years and was terribly lonely. For the first time, I had my own home, cooked, and every day waited for my husband whose work brought in living expenses. You cannot imagine how happy I was. Anyway, we started newly married life like this.

I had always worked in a hospital for my livelihood; now, I was married, and for the first time, I was cooking for someone. There were many "firsts" in the early days. For example, I learned much about cooking from my landlord and tried to cook various dishes, but not always successfully. I principally cooked the Japanese food I had learned to prepare at school. Taigin ate everything, and with appreciation—for which I was very thankful. In Korea, the end of October begins the *kimchi* season. *Kimchi* is well-preserved pickles that would feed a family through the winter until the following spring. In the vegetable market, tons of *hakusai* (Chinese cabbage), hot peppers, salted shrimp, and other *kimchi* ingredients were brought in by trucks that filled the streets. Many people rushed to the market with their carts to buy these ingredients, so the market was in chaos. My landlord's family bought 300 *hakusai*, and daikon radishes to prepare the *kimchi,* and I helped them to do so. Often, neighbors helped one another to make *kimchi*, and it is the custom to treat such neighbors with the freshly-made dish when the work was done. It was a nice custom, which I enjoyed. Also as a "first," I, myself, bought eight *hakusai* and made *kimchi* for the coming winter. Now, *kimchi* is sold everywhere, but at that time, it was considered a homemade food and was not for sale commercially anywhere.

The reason I had chosen to rent the room in which we lived was its proximity to the hospital. I had been planning to open my own midwife practice, and I hung a large sign outside our house indicating my availability. I had a midwife's birth kit, and if anything untoward happened, I could ask Dr. Seo's assistance. I had no patients at the beginning and worried every day. I understand now that I should have placed advertisements in the newspapers or magazines instead of relying on one sign out front. It simply wasn't enough to attract patients. I don't remember how long it was after I'd hung my "shingle" that I finally had my first patient. It was midnight when a pregnant woman's husband, breathing hard in agitation, came to my home, pleading, "Doctor, come quick!" (As it happened, this was one of the easiest births I had ever assisted—the infant slid out still within the amniotic sac membrane.)

Seizing my kit, I followed the husband to his house, running all the way. No sooner did I enter, when the family shouted that the baby had been born and I thought I was too late to help, but I opened the door to the mother's room and looked for the neonate. It wasn't there! What I discovered was the amniotic sac with the infant inside. The mother-in-law caught her breath in shock at the sight of it. I didn't even have time to open my birthing kit, so I broke the sac with my fingers. As I removed the newborn, he began crying loudly and everyone there was so pleased that he was a healthy baby. I was happy, too. I took the aspirator from my kit and sucked the fluid from his mouth and nose, then I cut the umbilical cord to separate the baby from the placenta. I examined the new mother and she was doing well also. My practice actually began after this delivery. Most of my patients were last-minute arrivals who were too poor to go to a hospital.

In any event, my midwife practice was flourishing in Taegu City, but naturally, I became pregnant and suffered serious morning sickness day after day. At last, I was experiencing how powerfully it could control a woman in the first trimester physically and mentally. I felt seasick every day and no longer a living person. Simply looking at water or food was nauseating and I vomited so violently. Naturally, the sickness interrupted my practice and I don't know how in the world I was able to assist my patients in the birthing process. Nevertheless, I realized that I could control the morning sickness when I concentrated on the work at hand, for when I was called to a childbirth, I did help their long labor, if such were the case, and cleaned up the bloody afterbirth. I even managed to bathe the newborns. Of course, as soon as I reached home, I "crashed" and went right to bed; I had absolutely no energy left. Then, beginning the next day, my duty involved daily visits for one week to look after the new mother and her baby (after-birth care). Although I felt like hell, I took responsibility for that woman and the infant I had delivered.

One afternoon, a pregnant woman came to me for an examination. I was feeling awful, but got off the futon and examined her. When she left, I looked for my watch on the desk to see the time, but it was gone and I could not find it. I ran outside after her, but gave it up because there was no proof that she had stolen it. The watch was a wedding gift, the only one I'd ever had, and a memento of my marriage. I was very upset and sobbed miserably. My landlady was angry as well and said, "What that woman has done will return to her or her baby as punishment someday!" I still remember her exact words.

Seven or eight months passed and at last I was feeling well. I was examining myself to see how the pregnancy was progressing and I palpated the lower abdominal area near the pubic bone. I couldn't locate the baby's head where it should have been, but I was able to detect it near my stomach. My baby was turned in the wrong position. I decided to turn the baby back. So I went to the bathroom and emptied my bladder as the first step. Then, I lay down on my back. Bending my knees, I placed four fingers of my left hand on my abdomen next to the baby's head and gently "pushed down vertically." The baby remained as it was. I then did the same on my right side and felt the baby's head move a bit. I moved my fingers along the head inch by inch and in that way finally pushed the head back into normal position. I checked the heart with my stethoscope and again the following morning and determined that the heartbeat was also normal, but by morning, the baby was turned improperly once more. I repeated what I had done the day earlier and it was easier to move the head into the correct position this time. I applied an obstetrical binder with a towel-pillow to prevent the baby from turning back and to keep the baby in place. He did remain in place until the birth, but he was born with the umbilical cord wrapped around his neck. I sometimes wonder if it had been a result of turning him.

As I mentioned, my business was thriving, and I was able to rent another room adjacent to ours. But my good luck didn't last long. The publisher for whom Taigin worked was moving to Seoul, and we had to move there as well. I had dreamed of Seoul since my arrival in Korea and I had longed to live there. We were now in a position to rent two rooms near the home of my friend from Pusan. The rooms were much more spacious and nicer than in Taegu City. I was happy. The due date for my pregnancy was in September and I was *largely* pregnant indeed—I had a hard time trying to beat that summer's heat. I recall wearing a sleeveless blouse I had made of some cheap silk, but Taigin scolded me harshly, saying that a woman should not show her skin and that I should not wear it.

I was disgusted and was very disappointed in him. For the first year of our marriage, having a husband provided a certain degree of stability. But we often quarreled about many issues because our backgrounds were so different growing up. In addition to the sixteen-year age gap, we had a differing sense of values, although our arguments actually originated inconsequentially with an argument about my make-up! He was on his way home from work and I'd been wearing some make-up as well as lipstick. He came through the door, saw me, and churlishly insisted that I remove the lipstick. "You look like you just killed and ate a mouse. You look terrible!" I replied angrily that make-up is used to keep up a woman's appearance. I realized how conservatively he viewed women in general. He believed that a woman must obey her husband, carry out the domestic chores, bear him children, and raise them—alone.

One day, I asked him if I could buy a watch because I really needed one to do my job properly. The watch I'd received as a wedding gift had been stolen, but not replaced. First, I bought Taigin a watch and afterward said that I needed one and would like to buy it. His response was surprising, so I thought he was joking, "If you want to know the time, why don't you ask someone?"; but, he was not joking. I explained that the watch was necessary when I assisted at a birth, to which he replied, "There is a clock in every house. Ask the time there!" I was badly upset and almost too offended to speak, but I rallied and said that as I'd bought him a watch, it was only fair that I have one also. "Who asked you to buy this watch? I don't need it!" he retaliated, and threw the watch into the street. I looked for it later, but it was gone. I had made a life-changing mistake and chose the wrong partner—someone with whom I would never be able to share happiness and sadness throughout life together. It was too late.

My First Child, Haemin

I woke one morning completely wet in my bed. "Oh my God," I thought, "I've become incontinent!" Of course, it was only the amniotic fluid: the membrane had ruptured prematurely. It was 5:00 A.M. At about 8:00, painful labor began. My husband went to work, leaving me at home alone after he contacted my close friend and my midwife (we had no phone at the time). The labor lasted no more than five hours, but when he was born, my son's color was unusually dark, and he didn't cry. He seemed dead and I was all worn out from pushing for the last thirty minutes. I looked at the midwife, who had taken the baby and was holding my son upside down by his ankles. She then tapped his back a few times until he cried. Everyone was relieved! Finally, I could take my son in my arms. I was twenty-eight years old and had been a *primigravida*.[3] In those days, my age was considered to be late for a first delivery. Taigin should have been concerned for me, but instead, he had gone to work and returned at about four o'clock. The child had been born at 1:00 P.M. in the afternoon. My husband was happy to see our son, said that I had done a "good job," and stayed with us for a half hour, when he left for work again. He must have wanted to announce his son's birth to his coworkers and celebrate by going out with them for a drink. As I was aware of the dangers inherent in deliveries of a late primigravida, I was so sad that he didn't care about it at all.

---

[3] A woman pregnant for the first time.

Taigin's dismissal of the possibility of such dangers effected my greatest resentment toward him and each time we quarreled, I raised that as an example of his insensitivity. We were not able to resolve our differences no matter how long or how often we argued. There was no communication between us and he was careless about his family. My husband was simply not a family man. Yet he was not a bad person and really cared about the poor. In any case, my life was restricted by the law, and I was deeply chagrined by the thought that I would have to put up with him for the entirety of my life.

Holding my son, I mused that Taigin would be a stranger if we divorced, but that my son and I would always be connected. I believed that Haemin would protect me through all the years—a belief common when close, extended families were the norm. Unthinkable in my youth, nuclear families are now the standard, and I grew to learn that parents can no longer depend on children as we did before. Even though I gave my son life and raised him by sacrificing my own, he might be a very different individual as an adult.

I considered how I could continue my existence without being able to change the circumstances. I'd had a child with Taigin, and certainly didn't want to regress to a precarious situation. If this marriage were to be my fate, I would resolve to try and understand Korean culture and fit myself into his generation, traditions, and values. I decided to befriend the wives of his friends. The first were the Kim sisters. Mrs. Kim Yongea was the wife of Mr. Lee, editor-in-chief of the Tonga Publishing Company. Mrs. Kim Yongwon was her younger sister, and both had been to teacher's college during the Japanese administration. We hit it off immediately, as they had a sense of humor and were warmhearted people. I learned much from them, visiting Yongea every day with the baby and often staying to lunch. Even after I came to the United

States, we three kept in touch. We were like sisters and although Yongea passed away a few years ago, I will remember and respect her as long as I live. Her sister and I still call and write to each other, reminiscing about our younger days.

With best friend Yong-E, Yong-won Kim, and a friend Kim

The Hatching of Baby Swallows

Clothes washers did not exist in Korea when Haemin was an infant and I had to pump ice-cold water to wash about ten cloth diapers a day. The baby vomited each time he nursed, so washing dirty diapers was a major and time-consuming part of raising him. Every time I changed the diaper, he defecated again. I was a midwife, but I didn't know that this was the best proof of his well-being. Following Haemin's birth, my mother-in-law had come to live with us, which, in a way, gave me a certain advantage. That is, while she babysat, I attended professional meetings to learn the most recent technological advances in midwifery. On the other hand, I was unable to fit well into their rural culture and there were so many family events I had to oversee as the wife of the eldest son. I didn't enjoy Buddhist memorial services because I was a hardcore realist, but I did do my best to learn from Taigin's mother, and I continued my work as a midwife, hiring a young maid to help at home.

My second pregnancy, three years later, was not quite as awful as the first, but I still had morning sickness and the delivery was more difficult. Shortly after my daughter was born, I noticed seven baby swallows hatch and eventually fly away from their nest under the eaves of my house. I could see the nest from where I lay. I'd had only one baby at a time, I thought to myself, but the swallow had seven and its reproductive speed was seven times faster than mine. I watched them grow as the mother swallow flew off in all directions to bring food to them. She hadn't the time to relax as I did; she needed to return often so that she could distribute the food evenly.

After a week or so, the hatchlings began to practice flying. First, they flew just a bit and returned quickly. As the days went by, their flight time increased until one day they left the nest and never came back. I thought about their family relationships: do they recognize each other as siblings, or do they know their mother? I tried to compare their lives with ours in the world of nature. When time passes in a human life, relationships with others become too complex, and I envied the simple life of the birds. Giving birth and raising children are part of the natural order of reproduction. For our species to exist, we find a mate, marry, and become independent of our parents, but this mode of survival can be either happy or unhappy experiences, affected by many variables.

One day, my friends stopped by and we were talking and laughing. I saw my mother-in-law reading a book across the room. She had left her own hometown, came to Seoul, and was now a friendless, elderly woman. Her body language was so sad, and the sense of her loneliness powerful. Because I really empathized with her and was able to earn an income on my own, I made an effort to ameliorate any sense of dependence she may have felt. I decided to give her the use of the master bedroom and also the "run of the house" except for our financial management. But when I tried to suggest some outside activities at the temple or church, her reply was, "Do you want to push this old woman out of the house?" I was taken aback by the negative response, but I suspect that had I been her own daughter, she wouldn't have said this. I knew that, like her son, she wasn't actually a bad person either. Nevertheless, try as I might to get along with her, there wasn't much between us because we were not related by blood and there is always a strain if mother and daughter-in-law live under the same roof.

Taigin's younger brother was married to a woman from a wealthy family, but the bride had a hard time living in a country house, bound by the old customs, and sharing the space with her mother-in-law. I lived with my mother-in law more than ten years and it was a good life experience. I learned from it, however, that I could *never* bother my children and *never* depend on them. Now, since my second marriage, I have been living my own life, although I do want to see them. I want to speak to them on the phone. Over time, I've discovered that today, in nuclear families, children are too busy leading their own lives to think about their parents. That is the reality of our modern culture and it is important that we adapt to it. Worrying about children is a parent's job—we *can't stop* thinking about them. I don't believe that swallows experience such complicated emotions.

Growing

In 1963, I was appointed the chairperson of the Korean Midwife Association. It was a surprise. Initially, I declined the appointment because my Korean language skills were not good enough, but my colleagues and friends prodded me until I accepted the position. They believed I could do what was needed and do it well. Still, I was very nervous, because in one year I had to read the records of the previous conference at the annual association meeting, which all board members in Korea would attend. I don't know why I, language handicapped, was chosen for that role, although, I was feeling good about myself. There were also weekly board meetings that I had to chair, and these meetings taught me a great deal so that I grew both as a midwife and a human being. The annual meeting date was drawing near, so I practiced in front of the mirror every day, hoping I would not embarrass myself.

At last, the day arrived. Officials from the Ministry of Health and Welfare and about 100 board members of the association's local bureaus were gathered together. I looked directly into their eyes and did my job with confidence. First, I read the minutes of the previous year's committee procedures. I read it smoothly and the minutes were accepted as accurate. The experience taught me that I could do anything if I bent my mind to it. The technology of tape recording or computerized data were not yet available, as they now are. The minutes had to be handwritten, but it was not as difficult as I had feared and I was able to complete my tasks without any trouble.

I chaired two consecutive annual meetings and was appointed again for a third year, but that time, I declined and could not be persuaded otherwise. I needed more time for myself and I had already received certain benefits from the years during which I served. I was now able to obtain data more rapidly than my colleagues, and I could attend a number of research-committee meetings as well. I believe I have already acknowledged that Korea was behind the times both culturally and technologically, so I needed to attend many lectures to catch up with the rest of the world. One lecture was offered by the American Red Cross; and another, actually, a two-week seminar, was held by a Korean nurse who lived in the United States. After the seminar, each attendee was given a birthing kit packaged in an aluminum case as a souvenir from America. It amazed me that we received so nice a kit free of charge. Both the lectures and the kit were very useful for my later career, particularly in the United States, although I never imagined going to the States at that point. Beyond furthering my midwifery education, the phrase

財團法人大韓助產婦協會十四回定期總會記念
1963. 4. 17.

With group at Korean Midwifery seminar. I was nominated chairman of the
general council in 1963.

"family planning" was becoming popular and I was certified as one of the earliest family-planning instructors. I visited a great many locations, such as factories, and lectured on the benefits of contraception to the female workers.

With group at American Red Cross seminar

My financial situation was improving, but it was difficult for me as a married woman to send money to my mother on Cheju Island as I wished. I was constantly worried about her, for every time I sent her a small amount of cash, she sent me some food—such as dried fish—in return. Indeed, she died of malnutrition. I wish I had done more for her, but it is too late. I think I am among many people who feel the same way about their mothers. It is said, "When we want to take care of parents, parents are no longer waiting." Mothers feel un-conditional love for their children, and it was only after I had become a mother and reached her age that I understood how she must have felt about me.

During my children's toddler years, I learned how to save money, Korean-style. There, a large number of people save their money via a system called a *susu* (a pool that is contracted or pledged). Various types of *susu* exist, but all have a captain and a group was formed among individuals who trust one another. The captain had to be a respected person, or no one would have joined the group. The *susu* process is as follows: initially, money is gathered from the pool members and someone who has an immediate need uses it. The borrower pays the money back in installments until the principal and the interest are repaid. The captain has the advantage of choosing to be the first to withdraw funds, but has responsibility for the entire group. The amount contributed depends on the financial level of the members, and groups are formed by individuals in similar financial conditions. I have read a newspaper article reporting that a *susu* formed by some politicians' wives failed, and that the principal was a few million wone! Yet, this system is normally better than dealing with banks if the captain and the members are trustworthy. However, the government did not encourage this practice because it didn't contribute to the Korean economy. I joined a *susu* as well, and was able to buy our house. After I emigrated to the United States, a *susu* again helped me to save money for a condominium in Fort Lee, New Jersey.

A New Enterprise

We bought our first house in the Seudemun borough on a residential street and I hung a large shingle, "Midwife Practice," in front. But I had no patients and I feared that the era of midwifery was over. Again, I gave great thought to another way, a new way, of earning an income. The result was that I opened a beauty salon, using a corner room in our new house. I'd discovered that American women try to care for themselves in such a way that they remain beautiful even at an advanced age. I admired their positive thinking and hoped to be like them. I had my husband's approval to study at beauty school for one year in order to open my own salon. Soon, I registered, and my friend, Mrs. Kim Yongwon, also interested in the school, registered with me. We went to school together for the year and found it a lot of fun. I practiced making hair curly using a charcoal-heated iron and a wooden board on which real hair was glued. My skill at graduation was far from a level where I could do decent work on a client, but I had enrolled in the school solely to get a license for my salon. I wasn't terribly interested in my capabilities as a hairdresser. I hired a professional stylist and was open for business, but she quit soon afterward because I hadn't any customers. I hired another stylist and this time a few clients began patronizing my shop. However, after paying the hairdresser and settling my business expenses, there wasn't much left as profit. One year later, I closed the salon without hesitation.

By then, Taigin had already left his job at the publisher's and had established his own business, the Chong Un Publishing Company. There were about four or five employees including my nephew, who had returned from Japan with me. It seemed as though I would be the wife of a company president who could simply enjoy life, but in reality, I was obliged to work there as an accountant. Our life was not easy, but once we owned the house, we were able to update and sell it profitably, and buy a better one. Our second house, where my mother-in-law died after many years, was built in the Japanese style, had a large living room and a kitchen, two large rooms on the second floor, and also a detached cottage separate from the main building for a tenant if we chose to rent it for extra money. I became friendly with the family of four who did rent it and we have remained friends ever since (forty years).

Luckily, my husband was too busy running his company to notice, so I was able to install a modern kitchen and bathroom in place of the old-fashioned ones we found. Nevertheless, he was not happy that I spent money and time on the house rather than on the company, and this was often the source of our quarrels. We were better off financially, but Taigin's lack of interest in his family persisted. A family trip was a dream in a dream: I begged him for months to come with us on a picnic and finally resorted to a series of arguments. So he agreed, leaving early to return to work.

He worked from early morning until late at night every day to bring his dream to fruition—the dream of publishing a world atlas/reference volume filled with photos. He intended to offer the Korean public a view of the world (literally and figuratively) that was absent from their education. This was a very big project and explained foreign cultures around the world in an eight-volume hardcover series. The problem was economic: he didn't have the money to publish the series, but he hadn't discussed it with me until after he'd started work on it. His company relied on the income from two school textbooks that were sold through other publishers, and from other types of books sold directly to book stores. I was never made aware of the specific cost of the project, but he told me that it would be a sure success. "The sale will not only pay off our debt, but also provide a lot of profit. Ask your *susu* friends and borrow some money."

I had to help him; the project was already in the "pipeline." I had to ask my friends for the money and I felt wretched doing so. It was not the first time he had put me in that situation and I had run away from home previously, spending the night in a hotel because I couldn't bear it. You may be certain that he never came to bring me home; suddenly it flashed into my mind: a picture of two little chickens running around looking for mommy. I returned only because of my concern for the children. I was coerced into surrendering my self-respect and I came back crushed and miserable. To this day, I wonder that he didn't come for me. He might have expected that I would return for the children, or he thought me young and stupid. Either way, I doubt he ever respected me as his wife.

My son Haemin and daughter Yusun

Child Care

When my son was about to attend kindergarten, the role of midwives in Korea was changing; hospital deliveries became popular and only a few women chose home deliveries attended by a midwife. Because Haemin's education was my primary concern, I didn't spend much time repining my practice. I wanted to raise my children to be the best, so that they would never have to experience the hardships I endured. At the time, there were few books on child rearing and those were written in Korean. I tried to think about what was important in their upbringing, for example, certain lessons had to be taught a child at different stages. If I lost that time, I couldn't fix it later and I worried about my parental responsibilities. What should I do, and how? What would a boy need to get a job when he grew up? I made a list.

1. To make a good impression. If he is handsome, he has a certain advantage. This is something that is not ours to remedy, but a good education can compensate for the absence of physical beauty.
2. To speak well in public. He would need the ability to make people laugh or to express himself in front of a group, an important skill in the workplace.
3. To have self-confidence. Not only must he be academically educated, but strong physically.
4. To be sociable and succeed in marriage. He should have various interests and hobbies to be well-rounded.

Of these attributes, public speaking was beyond my ability to teach; I missed the right moment. I did take him to learn *tae kwon do*, an Asian martial art, and arranged for piano, guitar, and singing lessons. However, it was impossible to convince Haemin alone, that is, without his father's cooperation to ensure our son's willingness. My husband paid no attention to the children's upbringing: only his business meant anything to him and I had to shoulder the roles of both parents myself.

Korean society traditionally addressed its expectations to boys, but I wanted my daughter to receive the same notice and respect as her brother. When Yusun was born, I considered what was most important for her.

1. A girl's beauty is important. She should be protected from marring her physical appearance in any way, and taught grace and elegance.
2. She needs to be educated. Her education should prepare her to be a specialist in her chosen field and to build a successful future.

I had Yusun vaccinated as a baby, the serum administered to the back of her foot to avoid a scar. I believed that ballet lessons would teach her to walk elegantly, but I didn't want her to love ballet too much, because the life of a ballerina is a tough one. Nor did I want her to choose her future at too early an age, so I terminated her ballet lessons after six months. I also believed that the ability to play the piano would be an asset in society and had her begin music lessons at six years of age. (It would be helpful as well as additional income if she chose to be a housewife and give lessons.) Fortunately, she was musically inclined and liked playing the piano. Even during the most difficult financial setbacks, I maintained her lessons until we moved to the States.

I made plans for my children and had them educated, but after I studied child-raising in America, I realized I had made big mistakes that I couldn't make right. The opportunity had passed. The old traditions counseled parents to educate their children strictly and perhaps, aggressively; at least that was the model I had been taught. Like other mothers who were determined that their young succeed, I ensured that my son studied extra hours after school as early as second or third grade. Korean parents often placed excessive emphasis on their child's education. Attending a "good" school was more important for the parents than the child! Methods of child-raising in the United States reached us and were so different from what I had learned. Assets, such as skilled public speaking, were inculcated by example or suggestion in the States, and I gradually came to understand the relationship between American parents and their children. Here in the States, through my breast-feeding education program, I've learned how Americans raise children and I have been trying to teach these methods, based on my own mistakes, to new parents in my parenting and new-mother classes.

Time flew by and Yusun was registered for school. Just about then, Korea's very first private elite elementary school was opened, with the principal and excellent teachers drawn from Seoul's best school, Tucksu Elementary. To be accepted at the new school, children had to pass an entrance exam, and once enrolled, their admission to a prestigious middle school was guaranteed. Many mothers were frantic trying to have their youngsters accepted. Luckily, my daughter passed the exam, but I knew the tuition would be expensive in the private, elite school. At the same time, we planned to move to an apartment. Apartments were becoming popular because of their construction and also because less work was needed for its maintenance. So, we sold the house and bought a unit on the fourth floor of an apartment building. In this apartment was a 76 cm x 65 cm poster of Paris, left by the previous resident. It was a scene of a young couple on a date, riding in an open carriage drawn by horses. Behind them was the Eiffel Tower.

I looked at this poster everyday and sighed, comparing this young couple to myself. Although I enjoyed, even loved, American films, they were obvious fictions. The poster gave me something else to imagine and I really believed that there could be a life like the one depicted. I wanted to save this picture forever, so I thought about embroidering a tapestry of the scene and having it framed. Quick on my feet, I made a copy of the poster on paper, then re-copied it on silk cloth. I finished the drawings, and brought the poster to the embroidery shop to select the threads, having learned the formal technique of embroidery years earlier. But it was just at this time that our middle-class circumstances worsened. Taigin had no money to see his dream through, although the series was finally published, but we had to borrow everywhere until it showed a profit. As a consequence, this stressful project destroyed my husband's life.

A Cardiovascular Accident

At the time, I wondered if the apartment hadn't brought us bad luck. Some believe that a house has the power to alter the fate of its inhabitants. Thus, one morning at 5:00 A.M., while my husband supervised Haemin's studies for an important entrance exam, he said, "How strange! I feel as if I'm drunk, but I haven't had any alcohol to drink." Obviously, something was wrong and I called his brother-in-law and my nephew, who was director of Taigin's company. Ordinarily, my husband's blood pressure was normal, but when I took it that morning, it was 140/100. He was fifty-three years old, and it seemed certain that this was caused by stress. I didn't know what to do, so I warmed his body with hot cloths and massaged his entire body to stimulate blood circulation.

In a short time, Mr. Kim and my nephew arrived; two hours later (when the hospital opened its doors) we were ready to go. We had to take the stairs to reach street level and Taigin grabbed onto the handrail. Otherwise, he could not have gone down the steps. Alarmed, I watched him walk toward the taxi and he was walking sideways, like a crab. He needed help to exit the taxi at the hospital. A doctor examined him immediately and, without benefit of further tests, said that my husband had a cerebral thrombosis. He was given a pill and told to wait until the X-ray technician was free. We waited until 4:00 P.M. For eight hours since our arrival, Taigin was given only a glucose IV and pills every four hours. By the time the X-ray was taken, he was already unconscious. Looking back, I am still furious with that irresponsible doctor who had so little medical knowledge. To this day, I regret how poorly medicine was practiced in Korea at that time.

This was the end of my husband's life as a healthy adult, and the beginning of another long journey of misery. He lay in a coma for four days. During that time, I frantically asked myself, "What shall I do with his debt? I know nothing of publishing." "What am I going to do for my children's education?" Sitting beside my unconscious husband, I could not think of one good idea and I could do nothing but cry. Even then, I was determined to have my son pass the entrance exam to middle school.

My husband finally regained consciousness on the fourth day, but he couldn't function at will. His lips moved, but no sound emerged. He slept most of the time for about a week, and after that, only the left side of his body regained motion; his right side was completely paralyzed. A month later, my husband was discharged from the hospital because he seemed to be awake most of the time. He was still unable to speak; however, I understood what he wanted because I was a nurse. For a while, it was not so difficult to take care of him, but as he recovered, it became more problematic and he often wept soundlessly. With advice from many others, I put him on a liquid diet, although the liquid leaked out of the paralyzed side of his mouth, nor was it easy for him to make use of his left hand, because he was right-handed. One symptom of cerebral thrombosis is the inability to control emotion and he was frequently angry—frustrated when incapable of functioning at will or expressing himself. I knew that anger could be very dangerous for a patient with his disease, but it was nonetheless onerous to contain my own frustration and stress at being the sole care-giver and household manager. There was no one on whom I could rely. Every day became a battle between us, for I had to earn money to support my family and repay his debt, in addition to my duties to Taigin, the children, and my home. Without the time- and labor-saving technologies available today, performing domestic chores, such as cooking, laundry, and cleaning were harder by far.

My only consolation was that Haemin was admitted to the Taegwang middle school. Taegwang was his first choice among the other top schools. In the meantime, Taigin was attempting to stand, but couldn't do it on his own. Rehabilitation was not yet a medically oriented practice, and I was so busy looking after our young children, that I was torn between them and him. Being my husband's nurse was not a nine-to-five hospital shift; it was my life, twenty-four hours a day, seven days per week. The truth is that I had been unhappy with him to begin with, and I wished that he had died in the hospital, thus releasing me of his care at home. But I could not escape the reality of my position and I railed bitterly at the God who set me on that road. What had I done to deserve this? Now I think I just needed time to adjust myself to the circumstances, which became even worse.

I tried to repay the debt my husband incurred and was frightened whenever I heard a knock on the door. The hardest issue was involving my nephew, who had a wife and three children, in that debt. If *I* hadn't two children, I would have thought about disappearing. I cried constantly until there came the day I suddenly realized that this was my fate and it could not be evaded. Fate is not in our hands to mold. I somehow grew accustomed to the pain and, surprisingly, I decided to live positively, coming to grips with my problems regardless of the severe circumstances. I can see now that I did, but I really couldn't then.

I had heard of many instances in which care-givers themselves became sick, and knew I had to do something immediate to reduce the level of my stress. I recalled my embroidery project of that poster in Paris. Sitting beside him, I put in one stitch at a time, imagining the young couple in the picture. I wondered if I would be reborn to have another life. If I could, I would have liked to have a life like theirs. I prayed for my dream and attempted to avoid dwelling on my harsh reality. I didn't think my prayer was heard and I certainly never imagined that one day I would be standing on that very spot. I worked on the embroidery every day as if I were possessed. Taking the edges of three thin silken threads between my lips, I bit down and twisted each thread in my palms to push it through the eye of the needle. I needed an artist's talent for perspective and size, and when the Eiffel Tower in the background didn't look tall enough, I looked at the embroidery board from a distance, then from below, and did it over again. I worked on the woman's face many, many times but for some reason, I couldn't make her as pretty as I'd planned. "She must be me," I mused, "so I can't make her pretty." While at work on the tapestry, I often found myself forgetting the stressful difficulties I faced, and I'm virtually certain that the embroidery prevented my health from deteriorating; I worked on the tapestry for more than a year before it was done. Today, many years later, it is in an exquisite frame, hanging on a living room wall in my Fort Lee apartment, a witness to my past.

Grappling with Economic Problems

About three years after Taigin fell ill, he was able to walk with a cane. He took a stroll out-of-doors mornings and afternoons as a regular exercise, although as our doctor expected, his right hand had become completely stiff from paralysis and disuse. Our income, as I mentioned earlier, was money sent by a textbook publishing company every few months and from bookstores around the country, but that was all we had. Ever since he had regained consciousness, he

My production—needlepoint handicraft

My dream came true—I went on a trip with my
American husband

had kept the bankbook and signature stamp to himself, not allowing me to have them. Thus, I wasn't sure how much we had, but I knew that less and less was sent from the bookstores since his company closed down. We could no longer depend on it as a source of revenue. We could repay the debt only in small increments. The other income was unreliable also, because when old textbooks were replaced with newer editions, there would be nothing at all coming in. Something had to be done. I could not hope to get any midwife jobs in the heart of Seoul. Occasionally, I lectured on family planning, but it was nearly a volunteer effort and undependable at that.

Taigin, in his sickbed, was thinking about the same situation. Still, he was unwell and did not have clear judgement: he was easily swindled not once, but twice, and he told me this as he lay in tears *after* he had emptied his bank account. If he had been healthy, I would have left him on the spot, but I could not do even that any longer. In the meantime, the textbook company told me that they would make payments only to the president of our company, never to his wife. My rights as the wife of this man were completely ignored, and I had been used by my husband. I was so angry! I confronted him and demanded to know why he hadn't discussed the issue with me before making his decision. He replied, "I didn't tell you because you don't understand business. He looked like a nice man. I didn't think he would trick a man as sick as I am."

I answered, "Husband and wife are supposed to work together! Live as though tied to one another! If you fall, I, too, fall! You waited to tell me *after* your poor judgement resulted in that swindle and our losses. What do you think I am? Will you ever acknowledge my existence?" I broke down in tears, but what had been done was done. It could not be mended.

He began to sob, asking my forgiveness and promising to never take such action again. I insisted I keep the bank-book and his signature stamp, but there was no way our argument could be resolved. We decided to wait for the next textbook payment, but he took the bankbook and stamp with him in order to receive it, and did not return them to me. Later, in fact, he was swindled again in a similar scam. Not a day passed without an argument. He had two recurrences of the disease and worsened each time. To bring in something, I made rice cakes and tried to sell them; I attempted to import canned food and cosmetics from the United States for sale on the black market, and sold the items to my friends. But they were buying out of sympathy. It didn't last long.

My next enterprise was making box lunches for elementary school students and selling these in front of the school. It was a private school and its attendees were from wealthy families, so I hoped their mothers would buy my box lunches if they were nutritious and good looking. Nevertheless, mothers were not accustomed to that type of convenience, and I didn't sell one. Well, I gave the teachers a trial lunch each, and it turned out to be a good idea. Initially, I was receiving orders for three or four lunches, but, eventually, there were days when I sold more than fifty. I really did my best to make good meals and when I was able to sell thirty per day, my profits were twice my expenses. I planned a menu the day before and bought the ingredients early in the day. All the cooking and boxing had to done by noon, so I was busy in the morning, but had time to do something else in the afternoon.

Mr. M. and the Trading Company

It was at this point, historically, that Korea and Japan re-opened their diplomatic and economic transactions. From kiosks on the street corner of Myongdong in the center of Seoul, Japanese goods such as magazines and music recordings were sold on the black market. These were attracting people who had lived under the Japanese regime. When I "window-shopped" the magazines at the kiosks, I, too, felt as though I were back in my hometown in Japan.

There seemed to be greater opportunities, but until I saw a newspaper advertisement offering, "Private lessons for Japanese Conversation," I wasn't sure of how I fit in. This was the start: I knew I was capable of teaching Japanese conversation to Koreans, so I put an ad in a newspaper. I hadn't a license to teach Japanese, and I couldn't teach formal Japanese grammar, but I thought it would be no problem to teach conversation because Japanese was my first language. Many young college students wanted to learn it and I was good at coming up with new ideas. I focused on how I could make learning fun for my students and encourage them to continue learning. I taught only people who wanted practical knowledge that could be used in real life.

My class was usually a group of four or five people, but I did teach privately for those with special needs. The class size grew until I was holding two or three classes per day. I gave my box lunch business to a friend and concentrated on the lessons. Most of my students were college kids and I knew that some left my class because I was unable to answer their grammar questions properly. Feeling it was necessary for me

116

to study more, I borrowed a Japanese grammar textbook and tried to learn. I realized just how difficult grammar was even though I could speak the language. I became embittered at those students who insisted on learning grammar. A friend of mine also told me how necessary it was to know it when studying a foreign language, but I simply did not agree with her. *Now*, I understand its importance, especially as I had to learn English. Anyway, I had more fun teaching Japanese students because I enjoyed speaking my mother tongue and my income was greater than when I made box lunches.

About five or six months after my classes began, I was offered a position teaching privately. Money was not an object, the student said. She was a beautiful young woman of about twenty-two or twenty-three years old. Speaking in her Pusan dialect, she introduced herself as Miss. P. Her father was president of a large corporation in Pusan and she was engaged to a Mr. M., president of another corporation in Japan. She couldn't speak any Japanese, and wanted intensive lessons with me, which I gave her twice a week. In the first two weeks, she seemed to be studying hard, but I thought it strange that, as the daughter of so prominent a family, she was fairly ignorant. In Korean, she began talking of her relationship with her fiancé and my class became more a counseling session than a language lesson. One day, she declared that Mr. M. was scheduled to arrive in two weeks from Japan. She said that she would introduce me to him, and asked if I would agree. "Of course I will," I responded, "I am looking forward to it."

I was enthusiastic, having the opportunity to speak with a Japanese person decades after I had left the country. She also told me that she might be pregnant! I was happy for her. The day finally came and Mr. M. phoned me. He spoke the Osaka dialect that I used to speak as a child. "Hello," he said, "my name is M., president of the M. Trading Company.

Are you Miss P.'s Japanese teacher? She's told me a lot about you. Thank you very much for teaching her the language. If you have time, will you join us for dinner at the Savoy Hotel this evening?"

I could hear my heart beating and I answered excitedly that, of course, I would be happy to join them. Oh! Even for a little while, I could escape the reality of my existence and have dinner at the prestigious Savoy! I dressed myself up as well as I could and arrived before 6:00 P.M. They were already there, drinking coffee, smiling, and talking. I estimated Mr. M. could have been my age or even more than forty. Whatever his age was, he seemed very nice. Standing up, he welcomed me to the table, introduced himself, and thanked me for coming. It had been a long time since I'd met a Japanese person. I realized that he was bowing even lower than I. He offered a drink, but I chose to have coffee as well.

Mr. M. told me that it was not easy to communicate with his fiancée, and he explained how the two had met, which disclosed a surprising truth. He already had a wife and two children at home. Coming to Korea was a business trip he made occasionally. His company had a five-year contract with a Korean firm for elevator technology. A Korean agent, Mr. C. was his only employee in Korea, and the Cn. Company contracted with Mr. M. through Mr. C. Mr. M. wanted to contribute to Korea's development because he sorely regretted Japan's aggression against her. Their contract stated that the M. Trading Company would give 100 percent in capital and technical support for the first year, 80 percent in the second, and 60 percent in the third. After five years, Mr. M. would terminate his investment permanently. He had met Miss P. at a coffee shop in Pusan, where she worked as a waitress. Mr. C. introduced them to one another and they became friends, but he didn't speak Korean, and she spoke no Japanese.

This was completely different from the tale Miss P. had told me. Remembering that she had even said she was pregnant, I was confused and tried to clear my head. It was apparent that Miss P. was lying to me and I became wary and frightened of her. While Mr. M. and I were talking, she was watching us closely, not realizing that her lies were being exposed. I wondered if I should tell him that she claimed to be pregnant. I asked if Miss P. knew of his wife and family in Japan. "Of course," he replied, "I told her when I met her." I looked at Miss P., and at that point she appeared concerned. If she told me all those lies, she must have lied to him as well. Who could know what she had told him! Mr. M. was someone willing to help her nation, how could she be so deceitful? I wanted to alert him to be careful of her. But I didn't. I realized that it was my job to be an interpreter between them, and as an interpreter, I could not express an opinion. She was my student and what she told him was none of my business.

Mr. M. asked if I wanted something from Japan, and he'd bring anything I liked. Yes, I said, I really wanted a Japanese grammar textbook. Teaching college students without being knowledgeable myself was not working out well. So, I asked for the book and offered to pay him in advance, but he declined. "No, no. You don't have to give me any money. I will bring one as a souvenir for you. I will call you when I return to Korea." I wrote my name and telephone number on a scrap of paper, which he placed in an inside coat pocket. How could I know that this scrap of paper would bring me a huge surprise and allow me to give up my teaching classes? An old adage tells us, "One inch ahead in your life may be dark." (You can never know what is in the future.) I think it is really so. After a delicious dinner, I left as quickly as possible to give them some time together. It was just past 11:00 P.M. later that night when the phone rang. I was still excited about my dinner with a Japanese person at the Savoy. The low voice on the other end asked for me, identifying himself as a police officer. He needed to know if I was acquainted with a Japanese man, Mr. M., and could I stand surety for him. Instantly, I thought that Mr. M. was a swindler, and I regretted having met him. In Korea at that time, there were many cases of people being tortured for becoming guarantors, unaware of the individual's connection with the communists. I realized immediately that I was overreacting when the policeman told me that Mr. M. had been in an auto accident, had severe head injuries, and was unconscious. His company's name and phone number were found, but no one answered at that hour, and the Japanese embassy was closed. He was in the ER at Catholic Hospital, bleeding profusely, and needed a blood transfusion and emergency surgery. However, the hospital would not treat him without a deposit of 300,000 wone (about $300 at the exchange rate of the time). My name and phone number were also found and I was told to bring the cash to the hospital or he would not survive.

I was in shock. There was no way that I had 300,000 wone in cash. We had some money in the bank then, but naturally, the bank was closed. Nevertheless, if I didn't get the money, he would die! This was a man with whom I'd had dinner a few hours earlier. I did not know what to do. I was in no position to ask my friends to lend me the money; I was still in debt, but I tried anyway. Mr. M. was a lucky man that day. The friend who took over my box lunch business had the cash on-hand to lend me and she was kind enough to come to the hospital with me, bringing the 300,000 wone. We rushed from the taxi to the ER, and found Mr. M., wandering in a daze, covered with blood, moaning, "*Itai! Itai!*" (I'm hurt). It was hard to believe that it was the same man I'd dined with. He was frenzied and screaming in pain:

a 10 x 10 cm piece of skin with his hair on it hung from his head and his skull was exposed. I cried out his name several times, but the hospital staff and nurses said that he was unable to respond. We paid the deposit and then they began the surgery. I was very, very angry. I was furious. How dare they call themselves the "Catholic" Hospital, but demand advance payment in an emergency! Would they have let him die if I hadn't been able to raise the cash? I suppose so.

According to the police officer, Mr. M. and Miss P. drove to the mountains after I left and had the accident on their way home. Miss P. and the driver were brought to another hospital, and were treated for simple bone fractures. At last, the police reached Ambassador Tsuruta at his home and he rushed to the hospital. Giving me his business card, he bowed politely and said that I had saved Mr. M.'s life, "I will tell his family what happened when they get here and will make sure that you have your money back." It was the first and last time I ever saw him. I actually had no reason to be in contact with him, but for some reason, I remember his name to this day.

It was already after 1:00 A.M. Korea set a curfew at that time, and no one was allowed to be on the street after midnight. The friend who had loaned me the cash wanted to go home to begin preparing the day's lunches, so the police drove her home. I called Taigin and told him that I would remain at the hospital to care for Mr. M. The staff welcomed my help because I was a nurse and the only one able to speak Japanese. I tried to analyze the reason I was helping Mr. M., whom I didn't know well—no one had asked me to stay on through the night. Then why was I? I guess the answer was that I enjoyed the atmosphere of a big hospital similar to the one I had worked at in my youth. Secondly, I liked the fact that I was looking after a Japanese-speaking patient. I felt as though I were back in the days of the Hiroshima Sanatorium;

I wanted so badly to escape from my home, where I couldn't breathe, even if only for one night.

The next morning, Mr. C. and a Japanese employee arrived at the hospital early. They both seemed confused seeing me at Mr. M.'s bedside, probably wondering, "Who is this strange woman tending to our president?" I identified myself and explained how it happened that I was there, but they probably thought I was another of his mistresses, like Miss P. It was apparent that they were uncomfortable, but they thanked me and promised to repay me early the next morning. For my part, I was surprised and apprehensive that a firm of that size could not repay me immediately. Shortly afterward, the president of Cn. Company and a few employees came to visit the injured man. Once more, I explained the situation. "You have saved his life, and have been caring for him since the surgery even though you are barely acquainted," said the company president. "We don't know how to thank you enough."

I felt a bit less uneasy, but they ignored me after that. Only Mr. M. knew me, and he was still unconscious. The amount I'd borrowed for him to save his life was a great deal of money, indeed. I didn't want to go home yet, although I knew that I would not be repaid until the following day. I had breakfast away from the hospital and then returned there, but I wasn't comfortable being there, as his visitors seemed irritated by my presence. Mr. C., a Korean, and therefore not habituated to concealing his real motives as the Japanese did, came to me with an obvious attitude. He proposed that since I was tired, I should go home and rest and his wife would see to the patient. She came the next day, but spoke no Japanese. I had the feeling that Mr. C. was taking advantage of both sides—the Korean company and the M. firm—in order to make a deal for his own profit. I also overheard employees of the Cn. Company refer to C. as a very nasty man. In all likelihood, he had introduced Miss P. to curry favor with Mr. M. During the time the patient was comatose, C. could mislead everyone into thinking it was he who had saved Mr. M.'s life. Perhaps my imagination was overly active, but my instincts led me to stay in the hospital until consciousness was regained. So I did stay on two more days, returning home only for a change of clothing. He sometimes appeared to waken from his coma, but soon relapsed. In fact, I did have one enjoyable moment with him: he awakened at midnight and we talked briefly. I sang an old Japanese song and he began singing after me. Soon, we were singing a duet! I think he was my age, and I was able to help him regain a bit of his distant memories, which made me quite emotional. I even wept. From the third day on, he often drifted out of the coma during the day, but after sleeping again, he had no recollection of anything that had transpired during his previous waking period. His memory lacked the ability to connect one occurrence with another.

His Japanese employees arrived about then. They had been delayed because of the travel documents, but now brought me a souvenir and returned the 300,000 wone. One of them took me aside in the waiting room and said, "I feel terrible saying this because you have done everything you could, but his wife will be here tomorrow from Japan. We need you to stay away." I reacted with shock and embarrassment. What I had done was for the patient's benefit, but to these people it was an unnecessary kindness, and therefore, suspect. They didn't want the wife to discover that the incident took place while he was with his Korean mistress. I was furious because I had nothing to do with his intimate affairs.

I asked if he knew who I was and why I concerned myself with Mr. M. He replied that he had no information about me, so I explained the situation once again, clarifying my part in it and what had occurred in the past days. I believe he really had been ignorant of the facts, and he certainly did apologize. Then he requested that it would be very helpful if I stayed on, continued caring for the patient, and assisted Mr. M.'s wife, who could not speak Korean. He made his request official, and gave me his business card. When Mrs. M. arrived at the hospital, I related the history of her husband's progress, and taught her some basic nursing methods so that she could take over and care for him. She was very appreciative then, but her attitude was very different by the following day. In all probability, she had been seriously misinformed about me. I was saddened, but I thought it was about time for me to leave.

Mr. M. continued to recover day by day. As I write this memoir, I think the problem arose because I met him through Miss P., his secret mistress. His people were trying desperately to conceal the illicit relationship. Of course, no one believed that a stranger would risk paying that sum to the hospital; and I had also mistakenly volunteered my nursing skills when I should have charged the standard fee. I probably would have avoided an unpleasant misunderstanding about my identity. I regret it now. It was shameful that Mr. C. tried to implicate me in something unsavory because he was so anxious to succeed. I may have been miserable on my way home, but I was proud that I saved a man's life, and the few days had provided a little stimulation. From this point of view, I'm satisfied I did the right thing.

A month passed uneventfully, although I occasionally wondered whether the patient had returned to Japan. Just as I was still concerned for his well-being, I simultaneously tried to forget the entire incident, but one day, a stranger telephoned. It was the employee from the Cn. Company, whom I had spoken to at the hospital. He reported that Mr. M. recovered from his injuries and was about to return home. I told him that I was unaware of the news and hadn't been contacted for a long time. "Mr. C. is a devious man, but I can't believe Mr. M. is leaving without saying anything to you—you saved his life!" my caller declared. He was angry and offered to give me Mr. M.'s hotel room phone number, which I took. I was uncertain if this man had a poor relationship with C. and M., or if he had simply phoned as a kindness.

I made up my mind to call and say goodbye, but it was his wife who answered. I said that I had been his nurse and was calling to ask about his progress. She replied, first, by thanking me for all I had done, and to report that her husband had recovered. He had not, however, regained all of his memory. She said that he was being discharged from the hospital and the following day would return to Japan. She also apologized for not having been in touch, "We have been so busy. M. is here, would you like to talk to him?" Her words were polite, although her demeanor was somewhat business-like. He took the phone and said hello. "I've heard that you've done a great deal for me, and I will always be grateful, but I really don't remember a thing. I will rest in Japan for a while, but when I am in Korea on my next visit, I will contact you. Thank you very much."

I was quite uneasy afterward, because it probably seemed that I called only to obtain a thank you, and I was left with a bitter taste. Six months went by. I was tired of the Japanese classes and was considering what next I would do with my future. In the meantime, I'd been completing my Parisian tapestry. Then, unexpectedly, the man I had spoken to at the time of the hospital phoned to say that Mr. M. was in Korea, although this was actually the second visit since his recovery. I should have ignored him, but I was curious and rang him instead. My former patient answered the phone, sounding vigorous, and apologized for not having been in contact sooner. The first trip lasted only two days and he had

had too many issues to see to and not a moment to spare. On this visit, he planned to call and thank me again, in person. I asked if he were fully recovered. "My memory is still not perfect," he said. "By the way, if you don't mind, how about lunch together?" I felt as though I were flying in the heavens! So, I went to the Savoy Hotel, as I was directed. Mr. M. appeared as he had prior to the accident, welcomed me with great courtesy, and gave me a folding parasol as a souvenir of Japan. The negative feelings I'd had toward him seemed to be passing. Then he added, "I am still alive because of your help. I would like to consider you a sister. We have a big room on the second floor of my house in Japan, and I would like to invite both your children to stay with me in the summer. Also, tell me if there is anything you want or need."

He was very kind, so I asked if he could register me in the Vogue Knitting School Correspondence Course in Japan. I wanted to learn something new that would allow me to earn a living in the future. I was interested in knitting techniques, but there was no procedure for applying and sending the registration fee from Korea, so I gave him my completed application form and the registration money I had set aside. He insisted on paying the fee for me, but I was equally insistent on paying it myself. I believe he was sincere at that time, and that his offer was genuine. As we finished lunch and were about to say goodbye, Mr. C. came in, and his artificial smile gave me the bad feeling that something unpleasant might happen.

Months passed, but I had not yet heard anything from the Vogue School. I wrote a letter to ask about my application, but their reply indicated that I had not been registered. I was so disappointed. I wasn't sure of my next step, but taking a chance, I phoned the Savoy, where Mr. M. always stayed when he was in Seoul. As luck would have it, an employee of the M. Trading Company answered and I explained what had happened, requesting that he register me in Japan. I was really glad that I had given Mr. M. the fee. I certainly couldn't have asked an employee to help me if I hadn't. The man I spoke with apologized politely for his employer's lapse and said he would contact the latter immediately and ask him to file my application and fee. However, Mr. C. called later and proposed I meet him at a coffee shop to " . . . have a word about Mr. M." The tone of his voice told me that he was up to something nasty. I agreed to see him because I wanted to clear the air once and for all, but when I arrived at the coffee shop, Mr. C. and the man on the telephone were waiting for me and an awful scene followed. I had no idea what was going on, except that they were suddenly shouting at me. We argued violently for a while and I left there astounded and in anger. To this day, I don't know what went wrong.

Shortly afterward, my husband received an anonymous letter written in very childish handwriting—like a right-handed person writing with his or her left hand. It said, "Even though you are a handicapped person, you are the husband of Koh Namsun. You'd better supervise your wife." Taigin was furious and blamed me for the unspecified problem. The letter was just so juvenile a thing to do. I was amazed at how stupid one could be! It was none of my concern, but I thought that as long as Mr. C. had the right to manage the Cn. Company, its business would go nowhere. I was so ashamed that he was a Korean citizen. I wanted to forget everything, but some time later, I received tons of textbooks for a correspondence education from the Vogue School, followed by a letter severing any connection with Mr. M. How did things reach this point? How could these people misunderstand what I did? Why? I still don't know what was going on without my knowledge, but it was one of the most unpleasant experiences of my life.

A New Occupation: Manufacturing

Correspondence courses at the Vogue School were not easy while I had to care for Taigin and look after my children. I could only study in the little spare time I had, and it was hard for me to concentrate. In addition to my domestic chores and studies, I had to earn money for basic living expenses and was constantly alert to whatever possibilities existed. For example, each time I read Japanese women's magazines sold on the street, I was struck by how rapidly times were changing. I tried to imagine various schemes for survival, some of which excited me, while others were disappointments. I enjoyed lecturing on family planning and occasionally received an offer from women's organizations or from female factory workers to address a group. I was paid little for it, but was always happy when invited to speak. There were so many opportunities in Korea at that time, but a business required seed money (capital) and time. I had neither.

There were also many improvements needed in family-related practices, and although I was eager to develop something entirely new, I didn't know anything but nursing and midwifery. I had confidence in my abilities: what I needed was a creative idea. An idea came to me eventually: The plumbing systems in Korea were primitive—a pump-up type mechanism—but I predicted that flush systems used in Western countries would soon become popular. At that time, menstruating Korean women used cloths and reused them after washing. So, I speculated that sanitary pads manufactured from water-soluble materials, such as cotton-like paper residue, would be a successful product.

First, however, I would like to share one of my amusing experiences, The Tale of a Toilet. It is an unforgettable episode. My special friend Sumiko was visiting Korea from Japan and staying at the Savoy Hotel(!). I was grateful to her for having looked after me, and I wanted to buy some nice souvenirs for her to bring home. Shopping for the gifts was a time consuming process, and when I reached the hotel, my back teeth were floating. A security guard showed me where the restrooms were located, so I entered the one marked, "Ladies," and opened the door to a small divided room. There, I found a large, pretty bowl filled with water. I thought I was in the wrong place, so, I opened the next door, and found the same thing. I just couldn't find a toilet. I was much too embarrassed to ask the guard again, and tightening my muscles, went up to Sumiko's room. As soon as I saw her, and before even saying hello, I asked if I could use her restroom. There it was! The same pretty bowl filled with water. I was floored. What was that? Well, Sumiko told me how to use it. It was the very first time in my life I used Western water-flushing plumbing. What an underdeveloped world I had been living in! I still talk about this incident with my friends and laugh at myself.

To return to my sanitary pad business, I thought I might be able to get paper waste at no charge from paper manufacturers, as it is simply trash to them. However, once the manufacturers knew that it was of value to me, they became greedy. I had to pay them something. My production method was to cover paper waste with a piece of the soft tissue used for tea bags, and I ordered a custom-made paper cutting machine. It took a long time to arrange for production, but I didn't mind because I was able to escape the hardship of family life when I worked on it. Meanwhile, we had to sell our apartment.

Fortunately, my husband's office was still available and I used one room for my business. I hired several girls to make the pads, and also pretty paper wraps for disposal of a used pad. We named my product, "Lady Napkin." I had an inventory, but now sales were the problem. Those of my friends who were the first women approached were reluctant because they, too, were in poor economic circumstances, and women's culture was very undeveloped in Korea. They admitted it was a convenience but, "why buy it if we can wash and reuse what we already have?" Other friends bought the pads as a kindness and introduced me to potential customers. The business was able to grow in small increments because some of them appreciated my professional explanations of menstruation's physiological and psychological processes. When I delivered the product, I sometimes taught female biology and family planning. Monthly sales were increasing, but it was not enough

Getting around on a bicycle, I offered Lady Napkins to pharmacies. This was about three or four years after Taigin fell ill. He was then capable of taking care of himself at home and walked with a cane, so I could leave him at home and look after my business. Nonetheless, bad luck struck again. One of my employees made a fire in the yard behind the office to burn paper waste and it was reported to the police. I was arrested and spent the night in jail. My husband came the following evening and I was released. Then, although my business seemed to have "taken off" after this incident, an employee left a lit cigarette in the office, and it was completely destroyed by the fire. Because our materials and products were made of paper, everything was burned and some books in the adjacent room were also burned. When I saw it, I just sat down and cried. "Is this my fate?" Again I was arrested and jailed as the person responsible for the fire.

There were many people in one large cell, but they were called up one by one, and fewer and fewer remained. I wasn't called, and I wondered why. A cell-mate told me that we could be released only if a family member came with the bail money; otherwise, we would be sentenced to imprisonment. "Why isn't my husband coming to pick me up? I have been working so hard to support my family. Doesn't he feel badly for me?" I often wonder how he viewed my efforts to support us. That evening, my friend Kim Yongea sent another friend with cash to bail me out. I hated Taigin and I hated God. I cried continuously. "What will I do now? If the government decides to change textbooks, ours will be out-of-date and worthless. We will lose our only formal income. But I *must* educate my children." I intensely believed that one must have a good education to survive in this world. If I hadn't chosen to come to America, I might have committed suicide with all my family together because of a hopeless future. I was filled with ambition when my Lady Napkin business was flourishing, but I lost everything in that fire, including my will to challenge life.

Destination: America

I spent day after day in tears until, at last, Mrs. Kim told me that nurses were needed in Germany. Many licensed nurses were going there to work, and she suspected that I might be also. The salary was said to be good. Immediately, I began to think of going abroad. I wanted to better my life from scratch in a foreign country, and I believed that I could send money back to Korea for the children's education. I discussed this with my husband, who was more depressed than even I was, and was disgusted with himself for his impotence, besides. He agreed to my leaving without delay, and said as tears rolled down his cheek, "You don't have to worry about me. If you like it in Germany, you don't have to return here. I wouldn't hate you if you never came back. But be sure that you give our children an education."

I felt badly for him, but I decided to go to Germany and began gathering as much information as possible. During that time, I saw an ad in the newspaper saying that a Korean personnel agency in New York was looking for nurses to work in their hospitals. According to the ad, the agency would pre-pay the airfare, a commission from the nurse going to the agency over a six-month period. I thought it was a wonderful deal, but far from viable. I did not speak English. Earlier, I had studied English briefly in a few months, but I quit. I was without even the most simple rudiments of the language and I regretted that. One day, I met a nurse who also spoke no English, but was in the process of going to the United States with her family, using her nursing license. If she could go to America, I could do the same, I thought. I believed that the German I had learned at nursing school was better than my attempts at English, however, I essentially knew only medical terminology, and that was unreliable.

Thus, if I were choosing a foreign country in which to start my life over, I preferred the United States to Germany. Once I reach a decision, I am quick to take action. I wrote to the Korean agency in New York. Soon, they sent me an application form, which took six months to process. While waiting, I went to a school that taught the English language, and sorted out my household belongings, as I would most likely not return. I had mixed feelings of excitement and anxiety. I fretted about leaving an invalid husband alone with two teenagers. I worried about my new life in a foreign country where I didn't know the language.

There are so many textbooks and audio methods to teach English these days, but back then, I could not find a single English-lesson text in Korea. I was more than forty years old and recognized how difficult it would be to learn a new Western language at my age. After some time, I received a work permit from the American government, an H-1 visa. I was so lucky that my neighbor gave me $1,000 to be brought to her husband, who lived in the States. She told me that I could give it to him in small increments, as long as he received the entire amount eventually. It was a nice deal for me. I left $500 for my family, and kept the remainder for the preparation of my voyage and for emergency purposes. I was told that nurses in the United States work eight hours straight, busy all that time. I needed to be ready for the coming hard work. I had no idea of how the routine of an American hospital was organized, but I knew that I would need comfortable shoes to run around continuously for an eight-hour shift. I found a pair of white shoes that looked like rubber-soled socks, so I bought them (and never wore them after all).

Now, I was forty-two-years old, had no friends or relations in New York, spoke no English, and had no money. All I had was debt, an invalid husband, and responsibility for Haemin and Yusun. I was having headaches thinking about the payments I would have to make to the personnel agency, my neighbor, monthly living expenses, and tuition for my children. I also had to pay my sister-in-law for coming to my house and looking after the household during my absence. I placed all my hope in the New York hospital and was apprehensive of being fired as soon as my language problem was discovered.

The day of my departure arrived at long last. Well-wishers came to the airport, weeping, and reluctant to part with me. Among them was my incapacitated husband, who stood leaning on his cane, supported by his sister's family. I had had many conflicts with him, but he was my husband, nevertheless, and he had given me a certain place in society. As I looked at him standing sadly, I found it impossible to control my own tears, but I was even more concerned with the children. They seemed to take my departure so well: perhaps they were relieved to be rid of an exacting mother. The teen years are supposedly a difficult period, and I will never be able to describe just how terrible I felt to be separating from my son and daughter. It was difficult for me to leave my family and emigrate to a strange land; and there were some who berated me for going, such as the friend who said without hesitation, "How can you go to a foreign country, leaving a sick husband and two children behind? That is such an ugly thing to do!" I had done my very best to sustain my family without anyone's help. These people had no idea of what I had been through, especially since Taigin had fallen ill five years earlier. I regretted that they felt as they did, and I still recall their heartless words, which, at the time, I tried to dismiss. I took pride in my brave decision to go to America, and I could not allow their negativity to affect my future.

The plane rose into the skies and I could not turn back. It was my first air flight, but as I tried to look out the window, my tears obscured my vision and I could barely see. The clouds were so close! I had the impression that they were like cotton candy and was reminded of the thunder devil in the old tale. I don't remember any of the food served aboard so it must have been good. A beautiful flight attendant gave each foreigner an immigration form that would be submitted upon entry into the United States, but I had no idea of what to write. After hesitating a long time, I eventually asked a Korean man beside me to complete my form. Night fell and the window shades were drawn; everyone was sleeping, covered by a blanket. I closed my eyes, but couldn't get past the images of my family and friends at the airport, and added to that were my fears of what awaited me in America. I could not sleep at all. It was different from my trip between Cheju Island and the Korean mainland when I was younger. This time I was responsible for two children. Their future depended on my new life in the States. Looking back, I really believe that if Taigin had remained healthy, I would not have developed the strength to confront life's challenges and the children would not have the happiness they now enjoy. He was sacrificed by fate, but was our foundation. I was grateful to him and I grieved for him.

I must have finally fallen asleep for a few minutes when I was awakened by the bright light through the window shades. Passengers seated at the windows were all looking out, and I did the same. Flight attendants were busy preparing our breakfasts, although I felt as if I'd just eaten dinner. In fact, I wasn't hungry. Not having experienced air travel before, I assumed it was due to the time difference. Between meals, I tried to memorize English phrases, but I didn't know the meaning of each word, where to put the intonation, or when to divide the sentences. It was so hard to concentrate: my mind kept wandering onto any number of things. Outside, dusk was gathering again. An announcement in English was beyond my comprehension, but a young man in my row told me that we were flying over New York. I looked down. Below was a sea of diamonds in the dark, a grand panorama of the city from the sky. How beautiful it was! It was my first view of New York's skyline. The image has been printed on my heart.

With friends when I was leaving the Korean airport

Three
America!

Wyckoff Heights Hospital

We landed at JFK Airport in New York and the passengers stood away from their seats, preparing to deplane. I wasn't sure what to do when I left. I was to be met by a representative of the personnel agency, but what if no one was waiting for me? I didn't speak any English. I was deaf and mute. However, there was no problem going through Immigration and Customs and I found that my fears were groundless: the Korean agency rep and the Manager of Personnel, accompanied by the Director of Nursing, and a head nurse were standing at the exit with a large flag reading "Wyckoff Heights Hospital." To my surprise, I was not the only one being greeted—fourteen other young Korean nurses had gathered beneath the flag.

We introduced ourselves briefly there, and then drove off in a small van going to the Wyckoff Heights Hospital in Brooklyn, New York. I couldn't see well out the window because it was already dark, but I could observe streets filled with soot and dirty pieces of paper everywhere. My immediate reaction was, "This is dirty! Is this really New York?" I learned later that Brooklyn was not an area where taxi drivers chose to drive, but it was the location of my workplace, the hospital. When we arrived, we were taken to the dormitory and each of us was assigned a private room with a small closet and a window. A single-sized bed and a desk took up most of the space. The bathrooms that we would share were in the hallway. When I was a child in elementary school, I dreamt of having a room just like this. It was, indeed, more than enough for me.

I don't know of any reason it should be so, but, believe it or not, the realization that I had come to America struck me for the first time when I used the restroom! My heart was full—my emotions, profound. It seemed that my life in Korea and my two children existed only in a dream. Now, after more than thirty years, I still remember that strange feeling.

I will do my best, starting tomorrow, I said to myself, but I had no idea of *how* to do my best. I thought I should get some sleep, since I had scarcely slept the night before; yet, the harder I tried, the more difficult it became to fall asleep. I dropped off near morning and had barely closed my eyes when I needed to begin the day again. The shower did nothing to rouse me as I had hoped it would: I still felt very sleepy. In the cafeteria, I breakfasted with fifteen other young nurses, but the food didn't taste good at all—my drowsiness seemed to overshadow everything else. Breakfast was followed by rounds with our instructor, who would train us in each ward over a six-month period. That morning, I saw American patients for the first time in my life. Most were old people with big noses, cartoon characters to my eyes, and it was probably the first time they saw a group of Asian people with flat noses. They stared at us as if seeing some strange creatures.

In the lecture rooms, the instructors began their orientation classes. They must have talked about important matters, but it meant nothing to my "deaf ears." I was thinking something like, "Can they see with those blue eyes?" It was just like watching film stars. The other nurses, who were able to **read** and **write** English, could not really speak the language any more then I, so I wasn't intimidated by them. But I was so sleepy; it never occurred to me that a condition called "jet-lag" existed. Other nurses were also falling asleep during class, which, luckily, ended before noon.

Coming back to my room, I threw myself on the bed and fell quickly into a deep sleep. I don't know how long I slept, and when I awakened, I didn't know where I was for a while. Dragging myself from the bed, I looked out of the window and saw a church tower in the sunset. When I heard people talking, I stepped into the hallway. It was the one nurse among our group who spoke English better, and she was giving us some information, that is, according to her, we were supposed to buy our own white nursing uniform and shoes and attend an English school. We introduced ourselves once again, but some of the women came with friends, while others had friends or relations already in the States. As most of these nurses were in their twenties, they had studied English in school and had a grasp of the language I didn't have. Moreover, I was the only one over the age of forty, which also had an isolating effect. They were occupied with taking care of themselves, so no one helped me with English, but I did try to be a part of the group and obtain as much information as possible.

A Language Barrier Again

We had been hired under certain conditions. We were given a temporary (two-year) Registered Nurse license and then had to pass an exam for a permanent one. Otherwise, we would lose our jobs. I needed a working knowledge of English in order to study properly, and kept a dictionary and notebook in my pocket at all times; but Americans' pronunciation was too uninflected to comprehend—I didn't understand anything that was said, much less have some benefit using a dictionary. The way to do this, I thought, is to memorize common phrases exchanged between nurse and patient, so I was constantly murmuring the phrases to myself.

One day, the call-bell rang from a four-bed ward and I rushed to answer it, asking in a feeble voice, "What can I do for you?" The patient who rang seemed surprised, and turning to his roommates said, "Did you hear that?" Well, my face blanched. I was mortified thinking I'd said something stupid. But the patient added, "You are very good. American nurses would say, 'What do you want,' That's not polite." "Come here sometime, I will teach you English," another patient kindly offered, and he taught me that after completing my care, I should say, "What else can I do for you?" Being praised by the patients was encouragement indeed. When I answered the next call, the patient asked nicely for a tissue. I didn't know the word "tissue." I didn't know what to do. Then the patient shouted at me, pointing at the tissue box on the table. "God dammit! You don't know what tissues are?" Everyone knows the word these days, but it was a new word for me back then.

I was being paid weekly: I think the amount was $280 per week (forty-two hours). That was $1,200 each month, a big salary for me. When I received my first wages, I went to the supermarket to shop for groceries. I was shocked at the size of the store and the variety of merchandise—so many goods and foods for sale. Items that had been sold on the black market in Korea were on the shelves. My eyes widened and my jaw dropped. I was able to buy a great deal for $10 and I packed them in a big paper bag to bring to my dormitory room. Compared to the cost of items then, today's inflation is terrible, but makes for a good old story in the good old days that I still talk about. By working overtime for a few months, I was able to repay all the debts that had so worried me. Luckily for me, there was a nursing shortage at the hospital and the administration was always looking for nurses willing to work the extra hours. I was one of those willing to do so, and I received time-and-a half wages when I worked more than an eight-hour shift. By working longer shifts, I was able to learn English faster and advance more rapidly in my nursing expertise, but it was hard work—sixteen hours a day almost every day. I was worn out physically and emotionally. My day began at 6:00 A.M. and ended at midnight. After a long day, it was especially nice to have the privacy of my own room, where I could moan and groan at will.

The other nurses and I finished the six-month orientation without a major incident. We had learned basic nursing care in a ward for internal medicine during this period. Then, each of us was assigned a specialized ward, and because I had been a midwife in Korea, I was assigned to maternity on the fourth floor. I liked my assignment and was happy, except for having to answer the phone. English conversation was difficult enough face-to-face, but understanding someone at the other end of a telephone line was a nightmare. I was *so* afraid of picking up the receiver that I placed myself as far from the phone as possible. Ms. F. the head nurse, originally from Canada, tried her best to encourage me in the use of the phone; she was a nice person, but very severe.

There was an unforgettable episode involving Ms. F. that I'd like to share. One day, she said to me, "Miss Koh, *go lu the centeroplay. Getta marmela.*" At least, that's what it sounded like to me. So, I said O.K., having, of course, no idea what I was supposed to bring her. My heart was pounding, but I had to go anyway. Pretending to understand, I got onto the elevator at the nursing station, murmuring, "*marmela, marmela,*" just as though I were praying to Amida Buddha. I was hoping no one would come into the elevator, because I would have to say hello, and that meant I'd forget "*marmela.*" Luckily that didn't happen. The elevator door opened directly in front of central supply. A nurse was there working, and I said, very weakly, "*May I hev marmela?*" To my surprise, she didn't hesitate a moment to say, "Okay." She had understood what I'd said! The next moment, she returned with a bunch of thermometers on a tray and, in amazement, I went back to Ms. F. with the "*marmelas.*"

I was still not quite certain that I had brought what she wanted, but she glanced at them and thanked me. Then I knew that it was fine and I was very relieved. When I recall this little incident, I freeze, imagining the worst possible scenario that could have occurred had I forgotten the word "*marmela.*" Just imagine if I hadn't been able to explain what I needed to the supply nurse—I would have been found incompetent and may have been fired. Ms. F.'s actual order was, "Miss Koh, go to central supply. Get thermometers." But "thermometer" sounded like "*marmela*" to me and I simply repeated it like a talking bird. That bird saved my career by a hair's breath; and I'm very grateful for it.

Wyckoff Heights Hospital was my savior. I had repaid the amount I (we) owed and was able to send enough money to my family in Korea. My next project was to study for the R.N. exam, and it was also necessary that I go to English school. I could not work overtime anymore. As I think of my experiences there, I cannot express my gratitude sufficiently to all the nurses, instructors, doctors, and hospital management who could have fired me but didn't.

ESL at New York University

The young nurses gave me quite a bit of information about English schools, so I went to downtown Manhattan to register for New York University's ESL program. Another tearful episode was awaiting me there. I took the subway to NYU alone, having a great deal of cash on me for the registration fee. A variety of people were in the subway car, standing, sitting, talking. Some were Asians, African-Americans, Caucasians, tall ones, obese ones, and in many different types of clothing. I never tired of just watching people in the subway. The train soon arrived at my station.

I found the NYU building and reached the registrar's office, waiting in turn with my heart pounding. The registration clerk saw me with cash and told me that they did not accept cash; I could pay only by personal check or money order. I was puzzled—I hadn't brought my checkbook along. They seemed to be telling me to get a money order, but I couldn't ask how and where to get it. I went to the exit and stood there for a while, almost crying. I had to inquire of someone. Two American security guards were nearby, so I asked, "Where can I get a money order?" They didn't understand what I was saying. One guard asked the other what I'd said as they looked at each other and shrugged their shoulders. Apparently, my pronunciation of "money" was truly bad. I repeated "mornee" many times, but they couldn't make sense of it. Finally, using a Korean and Japanese sign that meant money, I made a circle with the connecting tips of my thumb and index fingers. That confused them even more. One guard asked, "What is this?" referring to the sign he made with the same fingers. They were both bewildered, so this time, I took the money out of my pocket and showed it to them. That worked. The two said, simultaneously, "Oh! Money order. You want to say money order." I was so glad, and said yes. They smiled and made the circle as I had done, "This means okay," and, rubbing his thumb, middle, and index fingers, "and this means money."

I didn't understand why that would indicate money, but marveled at the interesting cultural differences. I was able to find a bank and bought a money order there, returning to NYU and completing my registration. I studied hard, but it was difficult to concentrate. Compared with the young nurses around me, I felt my abilities were slowing down with age. A year had passed very quickly. I was able to get a green card and wanted to bring my family from Korea to America, so I arranged for four weeks vacation from the hospital.

A Family Voyage

I returned home in glory. At least, that was how I felt when I flew into Kimpo Airport and saw my family and relatives waiting for me there. It was one year since my departure for the States. Haemin was now seventeen years old and looked like a grown man. Yusun was fourteen, a very pretty young girl. Finally, surrounded by those I loved, my long hard life there seemed to have been a dream indeed. Such a huge change had been made in my life since I had left Korea! Yet, I felt as though I had just returned from the moon. All of a sudden, living in the States seemed a dream, also.

I had to apply for the travel documents Tagin and the children would need, and arrange for our belongings in one month's time before returning to America. I thought it best to fly my children out first, following me. My husband was to come later by himself after taking care of the household goods that had remained. I thought my English would not be a problem at the American Embassy, though I was nervous and repeated English phrases over and over to myself. However, I was no longer tormented by the fear I'd had. Compared to the misery I'd endured only a brief year earlier, this chore was a triumph.

Time flew and the day of farewells arrived. With my family in the United States, there would be, for me, only my sister and her family on Cheju Island in Korea. At the time, I suspected that this could be my last trip to Korea. The loneliness, sadness, and countless hardships I'd endured there passed through my mind kaleidoscopically, but they all receded into the past and became only a precious memory.

I went back to work at the hospital as soon as I arrived, and suddenly reality struck. I would now be busier than ever. Principally, I had to pass the RN exam, or my family would be living on the street. They'd be here soon, and I could not live in the dormitory any longer. So, I rented a two bedroom house in the neighborhood. I prepared my children's beds and study desks, and even bought a piano for Yusun. I was so excited and eager for them to be with me. When they arrived at last, I took them to the supermarket and was happy to be able to buy them whatever they wanted. Next, and most importantly, I needed to enroll them in high school. I had many, many problems communicating with the teachers in my less-than-perfect English. I had been learning the phrases used in hospitals, but was stymied on this occasion. My children looked at me for help when they were questioned by the teachers, their facial expressions saying, "You've been here for a year! And you still don't understand?" Whatever they thought didn't matter. I didn't understand the teachers, period. I remember being in a cold sweat.

Nevertheless, both youngsters skipped grades because they were brilliant at mathematics, but their limited knowledge of English made it uncomfortable to attend school. Haemin, particularly, did not want to go. I wasn't aware at the time, but I later learned that he cut classes and met friends at a Korean church, instead. My husband flew in during the period Haemin was refusing to go to school. We had moved to America so that they *could* get a better education. I would not give up, but I was troubled and didn't know how to deal with him. The absence of a healthy father must have created a great void in his life. I never expected that raising a teen-aged boy would be so hard. As a mother, I had done my best for him. Where did I go wrong?

Life in New York

I still had only one year left to pass the RN exam, regardless of the complications in my family life. I tried to memorize English words, but when I thought I'd succeeded with one word, I discovered that I'd forgotten another. I would read a textbook, but could not concentrate: my mind wandered as soon as my eyes saw the page. However did I pass the exam? I don't know. But I did pass it on my first try, receiving a high enough grade on TOEFL (Test of English as a Foreign Language)! All I had to do was pass the general nursing exam, and I already had enough experience as a nurse and midwife to do so easily. So, I became a licensed Registered Nurse in New York.

There were a number of things I wanted to do after that. I wanted to do some sightseeing in the States. I wanted to take my husband to Washington, D.C. For that purpose I wanted to get a driver's license. That meant another exam, but it was more fun than the nerve-wracking RN test. Of course, it wasn't simple for me. I failed the test five times because I didn't understand the examiner's English and was slow to catch on. I finally passed on the sixth go-round. Once I had that license, I bought my first car—a used one. Haemin drove us all to Washington for a three-day family trip. It was the first and last family trip, sad to say. Taigin took sick in the car and had to lie down in the back seat, so I was in the tiny space remaining for many hours. That was not fun at all. For me, the pleasure of the trip was only in being with my children. Other than that, it gave me not more than the satisfaction of accomplishing an agreeable way of living in the United States.

Haemin and the Army

Haemin was still having difficulties at school, and I soon received a letter regarding this problem. It was the second time he refrained from attending his classes and I was very discouraged. I had serious conversations with him several times, eventually suggesting that he join the American military for its three-year program. I thought Haemin had no other options, but military discipline would at least place him in an English-speaking environment and he could return to school after his army stint. He must have been more troubled than I, and he quickly agreed with me, joining the army's engineering division.

During his military service, Haemin took an American name, Danny, and he graduated high school through correspondence courses. Following his army discharge, he met a beautiful and intelligent Korean woman and married her, both enrolling in college as electronic engineering majors. However, neither had any money. Danny received $400 per month from the army for four years of tuition, but that was not enough. He needed a student loan and also worked part-time to support his family, which included a new baby. He and his wife graduated with excellent academic records and went on for their master's degrees. Danny has been working for a major American corporation for more than twenty years. Those who know of Danny's troubled teen years are saying that his accomplishments are a miracle.

My daughter, Yusun, was a gentle child. Because she was three years younger that Danny, she adapted more readily to the American environment and the English language. In

Danny's graduation

addition, her musical talent was praised by her teachers, which gave her self-confidence. After graduating from Northeastern University in Boston, having majored in toxicology, she met her future husband, Bill, an accounting student there. She later married this pleasant and conscientious young Irish-American and like so many others, they struggled to repay their student loans and make ends meet. Bill's mother, a well respected high school teacher, was able to place her in upper-New York State's Marist University. Yusun's salary as a clerk was only $5 an hour, but the position offered good benefits, including family medical insurance and the opportunity to continue her studies. Like her brother, she too changed her name: she is now called Chris. While she worked full time, Chris studied for a second bachelor's degree, this time in telecommunication, and subsequently earned her master's. She gave birth to two children, and found a position as a computer divisional manager, where she has been for nearly twenty years. Bill earned a CPA license and has been the Comptroller of the renowned Mohonk Mountain House in upstate New York. Nevertheless, regardless of his long hours there, he managed to build their lovely home by himself.

Although I wanted to help them as they raised my grandchildren and confronted the stress of classes, difficult economic obligations, and new jobs, I could not do so financially. There is an old adage that, "Children grow up looking at their parents' backs," and perhaps because they had grown up in poverty, they were sensitive to ambition. Watching me study hard and work hard under any and all circumstances must have affected their own determination to succeed. I was very proud that both my children were able to support themselves and their families while they completed their education. I didn't have the ability to support them monetarily in their early years as adults, but I comfort myself that my choices were a good influence, and I will always be indebted to America for the opportunities this great country provided.

Chris with Bill at her graduation for her master's degree

Failing Health

During my children's youth, I was having an awful time at the hospital. Ms. F. had retired and I was being bullied by other nurses because of my poor language skills. In fact, one nurse maliciously reported me to the head nurse, accusing me of having dissolved powdered penicillin in tap water instead of saline solution! In all conscience, how could they have dared? But *why* was it so hard for me to learn English? It's been many, many years and I still find it difficult. Perhaps it was the three languages mixed in my mind, and I was also more than forty years old when I emigrated to the States. My brain simply could not accommodate a new language nor did my dictionary include American slang. In addition, I think in Japanese and translate the words to English when I speak, so others often don't understand me. And here, if one doesn't speak English, all one's abilities are called into question. Thus, I had to cope with many disadvantages those young nurses did not have to face. Regardless of the reasons, I will continue the study of this language as long as I live in the United States: I believe it is improving, if only in micro units. I love the message in this poem by Robert Frost, former American Poet Laureate, because it reminds me that my life is meant to go further and further:

Stopping by Woods on a Snowy Evening.
The woods are lovely, dark, and deep.
But I have promises to keep
And miles to go before I sleep.

With the relations between my colleagues and I deteriorating badly, I felt compelled to resign soon after I received
my R.N. license. I found another position at a city hospital
in Queens, New York, and moved to a house with a backyard
near my new job, hoping that Taigin would enjoy gardening,
but it didn't matter. It seemed that however I tried to accommodate him, our situation never worked out and we were
still arguing all the time. I guess his masculine pride was
undermined by his incapacity to look after our family while
I was doing so: this jealousy, caused by his illness, really
worked against me.

In time, my husband had a fourth CVA (stroke) and was
hospitalized where I worked. I think that the stress of our
arguments was a contributory factor to his decline. This CVA
brought about paralysis of his throat, a fatal site ordinarily—he could not speak, eat, or drink, nor was it possible
for him to swallow even a sip of water. An I.V. was begun
immediately, and two or three days later, the doctor asked
for my consent to insert a feeding tube. I turned pale at the
news. All the blood seemed to be draining from my head. If
my husband had to live with a feeding tube, he would not
be able to taste any food or speak, for that matter. What
could life mean to him then? He could receive the necessary
nutrients to save his life, but he would not be able to feed
himself through the tube because his right arm was paralyzed.
For myself, I could not imagine how I would cope with that
burden on my shoulders.

I felt lightheaded, nor could I think logically. Nonetheless, I had to explain the doctor's plan to Taigin. He wept
and responded by writing on a scrap of paper that he would
rather die than have the tube inserted in his throat. Acceding
to his wish, I refused consent. I didn't see any other options.
Since I refused to sign, he could remain in the hospital no
longer, and the I.V. was removed as well. I was in a panic,

and desperate, too. I feared that he would live in a vegetative state for the rest of his life. It had never occurred to me that he would be discharged and I had no choice but to take him home.

I felt completely alone. There was no one to talk to or rely upon. If I did nothing, I would be holding a funeral for my husband in just a few days. It chilled me to think that. So, panic or not, I needed to develop a method of feeding him. Filling a syringe with milk, I tried to put a few drops into his mouth. A few minutes later, I checked inside his mouth, and the milk was still there. He could not swallow and I could be charged as a husband-murderer if he died (or so I thought at that time). Five minutes later, ten minutes later, the milk was still there. He was obviously dehydrated, his eyes sinking, mouth no longer producing saliva, and lips, cracking. A wet cloth between his lips for moisture did not help very much. He could not produce urine. Over and over, I asked myself what I ought to do, and I feared that I would have to bring him back to the hospital and have the feeding tube inserted against his will. As I considered my burden once the tube was in place, I was overwrought that my husband had survived though mortally ill. I would not have felt this way if our marriage had been a happy one and I cried with regret.

I checked his mouth an hour later, but without much hope. It was a miracle! The milk was gone!!! It was already providing a bit of nutrition. He was too dehydrated to produce tears, but wept, inaudibly, nevertheless. Somehow, he had escaped another disaster. I dropped milk into his mouth again and five minutes later, it had already been swallowed. For healthy people, it is natural to swallow liquids immediately, but for Taigin, it was an amazing achievement, although my smile was a bitter one in response. He was able to swallow 240cc milk the day after his hospital discharge.

As I look back, his effort to swallow must have been unimaginable, but it also strengthened his throat and he produced some sounds, however faint. Of course, he was tremendously excited, and I was excited, too, more so because I was relieved not to be a murderer.

Taigin recovered very slowly and was capable of drinking from a cup, but as the right side of his mouth had been paralyzed to begin with, half the contents of the cup leaked out. Still, he cried for the joy of life when he felt the milk sliding down his throat. It was a long time before he could take various liquid meals through a straw and even longer until he could eat solid foods. Had we been in Korea with his relatives nearby, it would have been impossible to honor his decision to decline the tube. They would have forced me to agree to it and he would have needed someone to feed him all the time. He certainly wouldn't have been able to eat, nor would his voice have returned. Both he and I would have been completely miserable. I felt fortunate that we were here, and alone, in the United States; it was another reason for my appreciation of this country.

I resigned my job because I needed more flexible hours to look after Taigin and, instead, registered with a private-nursing agency. It meant losing my health benefits as well as paid vacation, but I was on-call for him should there be an emergency. Having my car allowed me to drive to assigned hospitals anywhere, anytime, once the agency phoned, and I was paid directly by the family of the patient. My patients liked me and the way I did my job, so that I was usually able to keep my clients longer than contracted. I even visited their homes to care for them after they were discharged from the hospital. I earned a decent living and worked in a variety of hospitals, but an ancillary benefit of private nursing was that I learned a great deal about American culture and what some of my wealthy clients thought about.

One day, my husband developed a fever and was hospitalized. I consulted a social worker at the hospital, explaining everything we had been through. Her sense of my circumstances was that I needed to respect my own life and she suggested I send him to a nursing home under the Medicaid plan. She was very helpful and saw to the application process. I can't express how grateful I was to the United States after coming here in extreme poverty. Taigin was moved to the nursing home, where he was given a clean private room with a bathroom. He was provided with the proper nutrition via soft prescription meals coordinated by the nutritionist, and he received speech therapy as well. SSI gave him a small allowance with which to buy things at the commissary. He had not only quality care, but also a certain freedom at the nursing home. He was no longer troubled by conflicts with me and must have felt comfortable and at home. Still, the hospital population was overwhelmingly Americans speaking English, and only I visited him—weekly, bringing Korean food. Poor man. I did feel very badly for him. He lived in that nursing home about four or five years and died there. His life had been made miserable by his illness. But all the hard decisions that followed—my emigration to America, the repayment of his debt in Korea, stemmed from the tragedy of his unhappy existence. Ultimately, the circumstances of his life were the impelling force of my family's successes.

Life is a long road. Married life is two long roads side by side. If one falls, the other is there to help rise up again. And so life goes on. If one falls and cannot go on, the other has the choice of leaving the road together, or creating the best environment for the partner so that each can go on living, but separately. Whether one will meet a new partner or not depends on one's fate. Only God knows my fate.[4]

---

[4] Quotation re partners.

I was released from the burden of caring for my husband when he went to live in the nursing home, and I wanted to return to a hospital that offered health insurance and paid vacation. Fortunately, I found a post at what was known at the time as the New York Infirmary in Manhattan. Shift hours varied from hospital to hospital and some had three shifts of eight hours each at the time; I chose to work the evening shift.

Labor and Delivery room of New York Infirmary Hospital

Private Duty and Hospital Nursing

My new job was in the labor and delivery rooms from 3 P.M. to 11 P.M. and my private nursing at Mount Sinai Hospital began at midnight. It was a long working day (nineteen hours including the commute), but fortunately, my private nursing assignment was often uneventful and I was able to sleep a few hours during that shift. Still, I was very sleepy when I drove home in the morning. I often just sat in the car and fell asleep in the parking lot with the engine on, yet I didn't feel it to be a difficult situation. My son was in the army and getting a high school diploma and my daughter was in a dormitory at Northeastern University. My husband was receiving quality care at the nursing home. Life was far better than it had been before and I was so proud to have been able to create it for each member of my family. As I drove along in traffic, I always thought that I was in accord with the rest of the civilized world.

The New York Infirmary was located on 14th Street near Chinatown. Three of the OB/Gyn doctors were Chinese and many of the patients were as well. One of the doctors had a large number of patients because of his special method for painless labor and delivery. Today, it is customary to administer an epidural for painless labor, but at that time, analgesics such as Demerol with Phenagon were used frequently. This doctor, however, used an additional drug, Scopolamine, in order to remove the entire memory of labor pain. During a labor and delivery, his patient was asleep with her cervix fully dilated. It was not easy to move an unconscious pregnant woman from the labor room to the delivery room, and neonates born by this method were often overly sedated, requiring an antidote. The recollection of that method still shocks me. Of course, doctors have the right to use any drugs they prefer at delivery, but delivery is just the beginning of a human being's life process. Many doctors probably don't consider that the overuse of drugs and instruments affect both the mother's and baby's future. Interestingly, the method was popular among women who cared only about eliminating pain from birthing activities.

During that period, I had a private patient, Mr. A., whom I remember very clearly. By caring for him, I learned of the prestigious lifestyles of the American upper-bourgeoisie and their way of thinking. I received a phone call from the agency one day offering me a late assignment. When I arrived at Mount Sinai it was 5:00 P.M. and the nurse attending the patient previously had been waiting for me for an hour. I had been called in at the last minute as a replacement when the nurse scheduled for the evening/night shift was suddenly unable to come. Entering the room, I saw a handsome man in his fifties sitting on his bed. Beside him was a Spanish nurse. After I introduced myself, Mr. A. told me that, as I was an hour "late," he would pay that one-hour fee to the day-shift nurse who had waited for my arrival. I was very surprised and annoyed and replied that I had been called at 4:00 P.M., and I was not at fault. The day shift nurse interrupted, saying that "We nurses cover for each other, so I didn't mind waiting."

Mr. A. had been diagnosed with myeloma in the bone marrow of his thigh three months after his first fever. The fever, which had been fluctuating, had resolved, but he continued to experience occasional acute pain and wore a plaster cast from thigh to ankle. He could not move an inch without help, so he hired nurses for a twenty-four-hour rotation daily. The nurse who had been taking care of him for a long time was resigning, and I was fortunate to take over her position for many months.

Mr. A. was a self-made man who was chairman of his own security company. He told me a great deal about himself. His father was a shoe repairman, and his childhood was a poor one. He had joined the military, graduated from college, and earned a master's degree. He became a professor at Brooklyn College. His wife, "Penny," who helped him achieve his great success, was a human resources manager at a major company in New Jersey. She was a smart, handsome, and tough lady, but eventually he tired of her strong personality and they were separated when he was my patient. He told me that they were to divorce shortly, but when he developed the high fever he asked for her help. She had been looking after him for the previous three months.

Penny was still in love with Mr. A. and she worried about her husband, who was in and out of the hospital many times during his illness; she did her best to care for him. At the same time, they bought a beautiful apartment together, although he allowed his new French mistress, "Stephanie," to live there temporarily. Of course, he kept this from Penny, but she discovered his secret and he was in trouble! He had only followed his passion for the French woman and I thought it romantic—a middle-aged man troubled with love. I had never been in love and I envied him being in a love triangle. He asked my opinion about his position, "What would you do if you were me?" In my poor English, I asked if he planned to go back to Penny, and he replied that he would not. "No, I don't think so. She wants to get back together, but I can't stand her aggressiveness." How about Stephanie, I wanted to know, but he replied that she had her own apartment in New York and had sublet it since she moved to Paris for her business activities. When she returned to New York on vacation, she stayed at a hotel. He had allowed her use of his apartment during his absence. I was relieved when he said that he did not plan to marry Stephanie, as it seemed to me that she wouldn't be a good wife.

"In my opinion," I responded, "I think you made two mistakes. You knew that you didn't want to remain married to Penny, but you did ask for her help when you became ill. At the same time, even though temporary, it was not a good idea to let Stephanie use the apartment you and Penny had bought as a couple. If I were you, I would ask Stephanie to move out and apologize to Penny."

"Well, maybe you're right," he said. I was amazed and so moved by his sincere attitude. He was an upper-middle class American living in a world completely different from mine, but he was so open, asking my thoughts, and even agreeing with my suggestion. I supposed this was due to parity between the sexes in this country.

Penny, who had a career of her own, would visit the hospital after work about 7:00 P.M. and would ask me about his health and thank me for looking after him. On the other hand, Stephanie came to the hospital about 4:00 P.M., bringing wine and dining with him. While Mr. A. sat in the chair, she sat on the bed, which I had just changed, throwing her long legs on it, and chatting with him, or watching TV. It seemed to me that all she cared for was to set a romantic mood. She never asked how his recovery was progressing. To me, the difference between wife and mistress was all too clear.

As I mentioned, Mr. A. was in a full leg cast and he was a tall man, so it wasn't easy for me to help him move from the bed to the chair. He grasped my hand with his, and placed the other arm around my shoulder, hopping on his right leg to his destination, and he was *always* naked. This funny incident occurred one evening. I was helping him move and because he had such great height and I am so short, my eye level reached about his crotch. He wore nothing except his cast on his left leg and each time he hopped, his penis bobbed up and down, up and down. After I sat him in the chair I'd already covered with a sheet, I wrapped him in that same sheet saying, "Let's put something extra to cover you." "But you are a nurse," he remonstrated.

"Yes, but before I am a nurse, I am a woman. I think the naked body should be a mystery," I replied.

He answered, "The naked body is a beautiful work of art." Again, I marveled at how our cultures influenced our way of thinking.

After he was discharged from the hospital, I worked as a visiting nurse, caring for him in their beautiful midtown penthouse and at the A.'s summer home on the beach in New Jersey. He and his wife had offered me a job as private nurse and naturally, I had accepted. This was work, but more like a paid vacation. Their summer house had three bedrooms facing the ocean; I could see the ocean and horizon line from the window. A beautiful, quiet sandy beach lay in front of the house and when the tide came and ebbed, leaving wave marks on the sand, I was reminded of running on the beach as a little girl. It was sometimes a distraction from my daily tasks.

Their stylish friends, those they saw only during the summer, got together at night for dinner and conversation. One evening, Mr. A. invited two couples to dinner and invited me to join them. Penny fried potato pancakes and I cooked *okonomiyaki* (Japanese pancakes). We were complimented for our efforts—Americans are so generous with praise. It was a nice dinner and they asked me many questions about my culture. I did my best to answer them, although my English was still imperfect. I suddenly thought of Mr. A.'s "naked" incident at the hospital, wondering what these people would think about it. I asked Mr. A. if I could talk about it, and he nodded, smiling, so I related the scene as though it were a big deal. Their response astonished me: they commented, "The naked body is a mystery," as I had said. "But, it is a beautiful work of art. It's up to individuals to decide when to be nude or not."

My nursing for Mr. A. ended after this two-week visit to the shore. He eventually divorced Penny, broke up with Stephanie as well, and married another woman. We continued our friendship until he died, although I had visited him and his new wife with my second husband, Larry.

Love in Mid-Life

One of my patients suggested that I change my name to "Nancy." I did, and I also applied for and received American citizenship. However, I was still having a hard time with English and I was still nervous facing different patients every day. I had no time to regret my fate, but when I had so much mail accumulating in front of me, I didn't know what was important and what wasn't. I wished that I had someone I could ask, someone with whom to share my life, and I wept often.

Danny, who had been sent to Korea with the U.S. military, phoned one day, "Hello, *Umma* (Mom). It's me. How is everything?" It was a simple conversation, but I hadn't heard him say, *Umma* for a long time. When I hung up the phone his voice echoed in my ears and I realized how much I missed him. He must have grown up by now. If we lived together one day, he would protect me, I thought. But the next moment, I told myself that he would have a wife beside him some day and the greater my attachment to him, the more trouble I would have with my daughter-in-law. What I could do for my son was to pray for his own happiness. I would use my energy to do something else and try not to bother him.

I consulted a lawyer and learned that if a wife and husband were separated more than a year, a divorce could be made legal. At this point, I had to think about the best way of living my life. Coming to America had been a big decision, perhaps a mad decision, but I had proven it was the right one. I thought that I was now reaching another point of decision. My disabled husband would not be coming home. We had never really bonded and I was never happy with him. I had done the most I could to ensure my family was supported, and Taigin was in the best possible environment.

If I didn't say anything to him when I visited him at the nursing home, he would never have known what was happening in my life. I wanted to focus on my future so that I wouldn't have to depend on my children. I induced Taigin to sign the legal document of separation by not telling him what he was to sign. I was fifty-two-years old then. I greatly lamented that few years were left for me to enjoy my life and fill the emptiness. The only thing of which I was proud was my nursing career, however poor my language skills. English will be an issue forever.

A year passed and Chris graduated from college, my son was discharged from the army, and he married. I wished him the happy, married life I hadn't had and I wanted him to have a nice wedding. Borrowing money from the bank, I arranged one, inviting many friends. His father also attended, in formal attire, after I had secured permission from the nursing home. He seemed to be very proud.

With my own family

168

Following the wedding, I was in my usual routine as a labor room nurse at The New York Infirmary and a private-duty nurse at Mount Sinai Hospital. Having two jobs wasn't easy, but I became accustomed to working a double shift. It became natural and I worked as hard as I could. On one of my double-shift days, a miracle occurred. A friend, Ms. K., declared, "Nancy, I can't stand that you live like this. Your entire life is in the dark. If you want to take a break from work, I will take you to a fun place." She helped me dress up and took me to a ballroom. That was the beginning of my new life.

It was a Saturday night, if my memory can be trusted. Roseland, a popular ballroom in Manhattan, was filled with people who were middle aged or older looking for company. All were well dressed, to appear as attractive as possible. We must have been the same. Standing at the bar we ordered wine and watched people dancing and having fun. Frankly, I was feeling sorry for myself having to work day after day to earn a better living. Unexpectedly, I heard a nice, soft voice from my right side say, "Hi, I'm Larry. What's your name?" I looked at him and saw a handsome, middle-aged man—a tall gentleman with beautiful white hair. For a moment I thought I was seeing the movie star Robert Taylor. My heart beat quickly at the sight of him, and I shyly told him my name.

"I am divorced," he said. "How about you?" I was amazed at how open he was, but I didn't want to talk about my life to a man I was meeting for the very first time. I put my index finger to my lips and answered, "Shhhhhhhhh." I can't remember what we talked about after that. I was entranced at this wonderful moment, the first of its kind I had ever experienced. I didn't have anything in common with this stranger in a ballroom, but he was rich in conversation and made me feel we had known each other for a long time. Then,

Ms. K., who was standing at my left, interjected, "What are you doing? Let's dance!" I felt badly that if I danced with him she would be alone, so I suggested that they dance while I held his wine glass. I regretted doing that as soon as I made the suggestion, but it was too late. They danced through many songs.

While I waited, a young man came up to me and asked if I would care to dance with him and I told him that I had a son his age. What a dumb thing to say! I wanted to take that back, too, but it was too late again. I just laughed it off. Ms. K. and I were the same age, but she was prettier, a better dancer, single, and spoke better English. She definitely had the advantage over me. Suddenly, I was depressed and was sorry that I had gone there. She and her dance partner were still enjoying the dancing, completely forgetting about me.

We hadn't had dinner yet that night, so I cut into their dance and suggested that we go somewhere for supper. He helped Ms. K. on with her coat and, taking her arm, the three of us went to a restaurant. He was the model of a gentleman and following them I felt miserable, but couldn't reveal those feelings, of course. I tried to laugh at myself, thinking that there was no way such a delightful American could be my suitor.

We found a Korean restaurant near Roseland. It was dimly lit and crowded with joyful diners, but, luckily, a table was found for us. We ordered Korean food and some wine. Larry and Ms. K. chattering happily, while I shrank into myself. However, one doesn't know what will happen in life from one minute to the next. A friend of hers was having dinner there also, and she was walking back and forth between the tables, finally leaving with that friend. Now, I had the opportunity to speak with him alone. I could talk woman to man, not nurse to patient and I was so excited, my heart pounded. It was then that he put his right hand on the table, pointing his index finger upward, and he said, "Hi," as though we had met only at that moment. I had never seen such an incident in film love scenes, and I was eager to find something to discuss because he was gazing at me so passionately. I found a good topic and asked, "What is your definition of love?" I don't recall if I said it properly. He then took a checkbook from his inner-coat pocket and tore off a sheet. He wrote down his definition of love, using every bit of space on the back of the check. He added his phone number and gave it to me. I didn't want to read so many English words in a dark restaurant. So I put it away carefully.

He told me that his name was Larry Cantwell, divorced two years earlier from his wife of thirty-six years. He was living alone in a hotel in Brooklyn Heights, New York, and had one married son. Larry was vice president of a department in a major merchandising company. He had a girlfriend in another state, where he worked during the week. His girlfriend was married, but her marriage was falling apart. Larry was thinking of marrying her after she was divorced. He told me all this very openly. He was fifty-nine years old. He didn't have the typical attitude of a middle-aged man who would try to show off his experience or knowledge. He was rather simple and straight and I was fascinated by his personality. We left the restaurant and he promised to call me. The word "fate" crossed my mind at that moment. I thought it was my luck that beautiful Ms. K. left us alone to be with her friend.

My life has been filled with happiness just by thinking of him, but he didn't phone me on the first weekend as he promised. He didn't call the next weekend or the weekend after that. I considered phoning him, since he had given me his number, but I realized suddenly how stupid I was to believe that such a wonderful man would be interested in me.

He must have thought of me simply as a woman with whom he'd had dinner—almost a passerby. I laughed bitterly at myself for fancying that I could be with him and I tore the check in half—the check he had given me bearing his definition of love, throwing the pieces into the trash basket beside my bed. I tried to forget him, but I couldn't. Picking the torn check out of the trash, I pieced it back together. Nevertheless, I couldn't call him because it was improper at that time.

On a Saturday, four weeks after I'd met Larry, the phone rang. "Hello. Do you remember me?" His soft, warm voice caught at my heart. He didn't think of me as a passerby after all. I still had a chance, even though a small chance. I don't recall our conversation, but I do remember with certainty that it lasted more than an hour. I really didn't have time to date, as I was on-duty sixteen hours a day between my shifts at Saint Luke's-Roosevelt (where I worked) and Mount Sinai Hospitals, but I didn't want to let go of this chance. My life had been empty and I wanted to seize this romance.

I started seeing Larry on the weekends because he came back to New York only then. A love affair that I had never anticipated began, although my income was reduced because of that at that time. I was sure I was doing the right thing. Money comes and goes, but it was doubtful that I would have a second chance to meet such a man. That was my rationale for continuing our relationship. One day, he wrote a poem for me:

We met and said, "Let's take a chance on love" . . .
Though you were wise enough to speak of future sorrow;
But why not savor every lovely moment of today,
Not thinking of what fate will bring tomorrow?

For Nancy, 4/3/79

I wrote a poem back to him in my poor English:

I find a big wonderful love on the street.
At beginning I thought "let's throw it away"
Though this beautiful love it won't be mine.
But it is too regrettable to throw away,
Attractive, warm and soft, but very sharp,
Full of affection, intelligent, delicate
And true. Let's enjoy with it.
Although what will happen next,
I will be burning out my heart.

For Larry
4/4/79

Hope of seeing him made me happy every moment and two months had quickly passed like a dream. Larry had a heart condition and was taking several medications for it. He was under the care of an internist, but when I took his pulse it was still irregular. He told me that he had had a heart attack on an airplane some time earlier. That worried me and I called him every day to see how he was doing. I thought that if he needed a heart transplant, I would be happy to give him my heart. I wanted so wonderful a man to live longer. I would not have resented giving up my ill-fated life to save him. We learned much later from a cardiologist that the irregular pulse was a side effect of the medication he had been prescribed.

One day he said, with a serious expression on his face, "Nancy, I am not focusing on a woman called Nancy. I think of you as one of the women I know. It's better for you not to get serious with me." Of course, I was aware of it. I didn't expect to share the rest of my life with him, but I wanted to hold on to this beautiful relationship as long as possible. He was as handsome as a movie star, full of warm spirit, very humorous, always making people laugh. In addition, he was so knowledgeable about everything, and could answer every question I asked. We communicated well, although my English was so poor. I knew our friendship would end one day, and that he had a beautiful, blonde girlfriend whom he thought he might marry, but as I looked at his delightful smile, I didn't accept that. I wanted our time together to go as far as it could.

Unfortunately, the day had finally come. He told me that he was going on a cruise by himself. I thought he was ending our relationship, so I picked up the phone and called him. I'd rather have said goodbye to him than have him say goodbye to me. "Larry," I said, "I think I must say goodbye," still hoping he would stop me from leaving. But what he said was, "I think you are right." The moment I heard his words, all the happiness I'd had with him vanished. I hung up the phone and cried bitterly. I didn't even go to work—I cried all day. When I thought that I might not have lost him if I were pretty, the face of my mother came to mind and made me resentful. After weeping all day, I came to my senses. I was rather happy that I would have so wonderful a memory of love in middle-age with a wonderful man. I concluded that I could live my life from then on with confidence rather than misery, and I was grateful for having had that chance. I dialed his number and said, "Larry, from the bottom of my heart, I hope you will meet a marvelous woman and seize happiness with her. I am concerned with your health, however. If you ever need a nurse, promise that you will call me. I will dedicate myself to caring for you. For you, I will be the best nurse of all." Regardless of this farewell, I continued to recall his warm smile.

One week had passed since he had left on the cruise. On Saturday, the phone rang. It was Larry! "Hi Nancy, I'm back." I can't express how happy I was to hear from him.

(To tell the truth, I had always kept a hope alive that he would come back to me; as if I could say, "It would be the mistake of your lifetime if you didn't choose me.")

"For how long?" I asked.

"Forever!" said Larry.

Midnight December 31, 1981

Courtship

Yes, I got him back by being myself—truthful to both of us. His former wife was a beautiful woman who had modeled for magazines, but they were divorced; and his current mistress was a beautiful woman, too—as far as I knew. But I won! I won him despite these beautiful American women. He must have given much thought to his relationships while aboard the cruise liner. He brought me a jade pendant from one of the islands the cruise visited and two postcards of the gorgeous ship itself, with poems he had written on them.

Postcard 1.

The cherry blossoms are far away,
The poisoned bird just cannot sing
But the ship moves quickly to my love
Soon, it will be spring!

Postcard 2.

The sea moves swiftly and majestically,
The ship is a small speck in all its immensity.
The myriad stars wheel slowly
In the velvet black above—where you are now,
Are you watching them too, my love?

He moved into my apartment shortly after. My dream life had begun. We laughed together every day and he seemed to be happy also. I was still visiting Taigin in the nursing home, Larry being very understanding. But I realized that I wasn't visiting him as often as before and justified myself by the belief that Danny and his wife would come instead of me. Gradually, I made fewer and fewer visits. I don't remember how long Larry and I had been living together when Taigin was transferred to a hospital with pneumonia, and he died there. Thinking back at his life, I believe he must have been pleased, in some sense, that he was receiving state-of-the-art care at an American institution; and he must have taken pride witnessing his children's successful lives.

Larry paid my debt for Danny's wedding and I no longer had to work sixteen hours a day. My schedule became lighter: three days a week as a labor room and delivery nurse at Roosevelt Hospital, and I was able to enjoy my new life as well. I sometimes wonder what I would be doing today if I had chosen my work over my relationship with Larry. I always conclude that choosing him was the best decision of my life.

Six months later, Larry gave me an engagement ring. It was the first engagement ring I had ever been given, and we soon married, Larry's son, Michael, and his wife, Sandra, witnessing our wedding. How happy I was to receive the ring and then marry the man of my dreams I leave to your imagination. Frequently, we dressed nicely in the evening to go to a fine restaurant for dinner, either Italian or French, with candlelight and wine and we always had pleasant conversations over our meals. One day, we walked over the Brooklyn Bridge together, hand-in-hand (after I took off my high heels). It was like a scene in a romantic film. Every day was like a dream: just like an Urashima Taro in the castle under the sea (an old Japanese children's story). Days, weeks, and months went by too quickly to keep track.

Larry always walked on the street side of the pavement, whenever we strolled together, arm-in-arm. His hands were

Visiting Nara in Japan after my marriage to Larry

big and warm. When we ordered at restaurants, he invariably said, "For my wife." It was so nice of him to let others know that I was his wife. I appreciated it so much. I no longer had to worry about anything. I also appreciated his ex-wife for agreeing to his divorce. One of my lifetime fantasies was to travel the world once a year. Our first trip was to St. Martin. There, I wrote a note to Dr. Fujii, the director of the nursing school in Hiroshima. I had been writing to him ever since I moved to Korea from Japan, and he wrote back, encouraging me over the decades. I wanted to tell him about this fantastic trip with my American husband. At one time, we were able to visit Dr. Fujii in Hiroshima. He welcomed us warmly and hospitably and gave us a tour around the Tower of Peace Park. We visited Korea and Japan together, but it was too difficult to visit Cheju Island, Korea.

With Dr. Fujii

Everything was wonderful, but my problem speaking English at work was my own problem. In the United States, July is the month new interns begin their clinical training. For labor and delivery room nurses like myself, July was, therefore, a troubled month because we often disagreed with the new doctors, who had no experience. I, among all the nurses, had this language issue and I couldn't stand up to these interns because I couldn't formulate an argument in English. In the worse cases, some doctors shifted their faults to me, as if I had made a mistake.

One day, I had a disagreement with a male Caucasian intern in the labor room and came home depressed. I don't have a clear memory of the subject on which he and I disagreed. I only recall telling Larry what had happened and he urged me to call the hospital at once. I told him that things should be left as they were—the confrontation was over. But Larry insisted—he was furious that I would be abused because of my nationality. Finally, I phoned. He spoke in a calm voice with the intern and the doctor soon apologized. Larry told him that he should apologize to me instead of him, and he did, very politely. I had never felt as safe and secure as at that time. I felt as though I were leaning against a big tree, after a life alone and unprotected. I wept for happiness, tears of happiness. As long as I am with Larry, who stands strong anytime, anywhere, I don't have to feel badly about myself. He often says, "You always act like you are nothing. Tell yourself that you are a person. You should live your life with your head high." Ever since, my sense of inferiority has greatly diminished.

While visiting a Korean village, we rented Korean national costumes.

An International Marriage

It has been twenty-four years since our marriage and I am now so accustomed to this wonderful married life. Eventually, I could even bring myself to argue with my husband over cultural differences or food preferences. These are unavoidable issues in any international marriage in middle age, I believe. It is only natural that Larry does not understand my culture no matter how I explain it because he has never lived in Asia.

Historically, Japanese culture has involved strict obedience to any authority: children must obey their parents; the parents must obey teachers, doctors, and police; and *everyone* must obey the political leaders. Grandmothers say that "a girl has to obey three people in her life: first, her parents; after marriage, her husband; and when she is old, her children." Another tenet is, "concern with other people first, then myself."

A typical aspect of Japanese culture is "*honne to tatemae*," that is, how real intention and ostentation are used. One of my favorite Japanese quotations is, "Even if I have much knowledge, I must not show arrogance; it is ugly and bound to be disliked." A proverb reiterates that thought, "A wise falcon hides his black-edged nails."

Such paradigms also influence the development of child care in Japan. For instance, parents tell children what to do and good children obediently follow. Parents kindly help a child do everything including feeding and dressing until the youngster is three or four years old. Parents sleep with their baby between them, and gradually only the mother and child sleep together. Dad sleeps alone. This is very common occurrence. Before World War II, the average person was very poor, but afterward, Japan accepted the conquering European and American civilization earlier than any other Asian nation, including American assistance to develop her economy. Therefore, the Japanese have never experienced the bitterness of a foreign invader, and are able to maintain their sweet-tempered culture. As a result, Japan became a great Asian nation. Unfortunately, however, this beautiful culture has declined among young people because of the advance of nuclear families and the adoption of foreign traditions and mores.

As compared to Japan, Korean culture is basically similar with regard to obedience to parents. A young woman "doesn't see anything, hear anything, or speak of anything during the first three years of her marriage." Child care is probably like that of Japan, although it is the grandmother who sleeps with the baby. But no one adheres to these traditions today. Geographically, Korea's location has put her at a great disadvantage. As I have noted previously, historically, many countries such as Japan, China, Russia, and the United States have watched for the opportunity to attack the Korean peninsula. At one time, Korea was a kingdom (from 57 BC onward), but the last, the Lee Kingdom, was destroyed by Japan, which invaded and forced Koreans to obey Japanese laws, and take on Japanese names until independence at the end of the second world war in August 1945. Nevertheless, many Koreans rejected the Japanese and fought to show that we are not weak and compliant; many were killed in that effort. Individually, Koreans are very smart, and as a result of our historic experiences, personalities have become assertive. This attitude has taken a firm hold on the Korean manner of dealing with others. When we speak, we do not use a florid vocabulary, but just say directly what we are thinking.

How to resolve various problems has always been somewhere on my mind. Which is more important, the ultimate happiness I have with Larry, or my foods and traditions? I've weighed them in the balance and I've decided to accept his tastes as much as possible. I try to order his kind of food in restaurants and also learned to cook the food he likes (even among Americans, he is considered a very picky eater). For Larry, who had a high standard of lifestyle, dinner has to be served in a candlelit atmosphere, and with wine. But I still can't keep up with his extremely unbalanced diet. I eat Japanese and Korean food every chance I get. Incidentally, I tend to gain weight, a real problem for me.

Larry had been earning a nice salary, but he had to pay $700 per month in alimony until his former wife remarried in 1983. Seven hundred dollars was not a small amount, but I didn't care as long as Larry was with me. However, he returned from work one day numb with surprise. He had been forced into early retirement. He had worked very hard for the company for thirty-two years, but the company was reducing their costs by laying off veteran employees and replacing them with youngsters who demanded less salary. I felt bad for him because I thought I had brought him bad luck. Seems that I have no luck with money whatsoever. He managed to have the alimony reduced by half, and Dale was married not long afterward, eliminating this expenditure.

He was sixty-two years old at the time, and still young. When he was looking for a business to establish, his niece and her husband introduced him to their gold/silver coin and stamp business, which he took over. He operated that business happily for nearly twenty years, dealing coins, talking with regular customers, and playing card games with those who became good friends. He retired from the coin business at age eighty-two.

Larry has one child, a son, as I mentioned. Michael had gone through an interesting and checkered youth, but he received a master's in liberal arts and, with the help of his wife, Sandra, then went back to school for a law degree, followed by a master's in law. He is now a brilliant lawyer in New York. Sandra, who is a lovely woman, and very elegant, recently earned her doctorate. She studied while looking after her domestic chores and they pursued their cultural interests with close friends who shared them. Now, they take pleasure in their pursuits, children, and grandchildren free of their previous stresses. They love both Larry and me, are very affectionate, and are in agreement with us and one another on just about everything. They have given us generous Christmas gifts of cash at the end of every year, which helped with our expenses. For these past twenty-five years, we have received fine gifts for birthdays, Mother's Day, Father's Day, and our anniversary, and they take us to dinner as well. They are such nice people and we are so proud of them.

When I was newly married, we often got together with Larry's family, but I really didn't understand their conversations. So I just kept smiling. In the back of my mind, however, I was thinking something else. Now, after all these years, I am able to discuss many things with them, although I still can't carry on a high-level conversation when the issue is complicated, such as politics. My English has improved greatly since I began living with Larry, but my aging brain doesn't seem to have the space left for new learning. I always think in Japanese first, then translate it into English when I speak. This has caused a lot of trouble. For instance, let's say I said to Larry, "I just spoke to H. and she told me she is divorcing. I am having a hard time to talk her into not to divorce. I need your help. What do you think?" In English, subject precedes and explanations follow. It is opposite in

Michael and Sandra took us on a one-week cruise

With my American family

Japanese conversation. So, with my English, he naturally understands that I'm talking about H.'s divorce. He would show some interest and ask lots of questions. But as I answered his questions, our conversation becomes gossipy and he would lose interest. In this case, I should have said, "I need your help" first so that he would listen to me as he prepared his opinion. I thought I knew the logical flow of a dialogue, but knowing and doing are very different. Nevertheless, I'm still continuing English lessons in the senior center, as long as I live.

Lamaze in Japanese

One day when I was working as a labor room nurse at St. Luke's-Roosevelt Medical Center, a pregnant Japanese woman was brought in in a wheelchair. I smiled at her and said, "*Konnichiwa!*" (hello in Japanese). She was so relieved to see Japanese-speaking staff in an American hospital. This was the origin of my Japanese Lamaze class more than twenty years ago. Larry agreed that I should take an instructor's course for a teaching certificate in the Lamaze method of childbirth. Of course, it was in English. When I did my homework, Larry helped to improve my skills, and my coworker Ruth helped as well. With that assistance, I was able to be authorized to practice. I was able to start teaching because I could lean on my husband and I can't sufficiently express my appreciation of him. A friend who came to dinner with us one day said, "You are an ideal couple who are covering each other's needs, and for that I envy you." I agree with her comment.

Back then, Dr. Terusada Horiguchi, now deceased, was known as the only Japanese OB/Gyn in New York, and he has many Japanese patients in our obstetrics department. It was convenient for me to both work in the delivery room and teach a childbirth class since they were both in the same area. First, I taught textbook breathing technique, as I had learned to do. But as I attended a large number of labors, I was able to study other effective ways of breathing and pushing during that period. Finally, I developed an original breathing method that helped raise the number of natural-labor births. My lectures primarily gave patients information

188

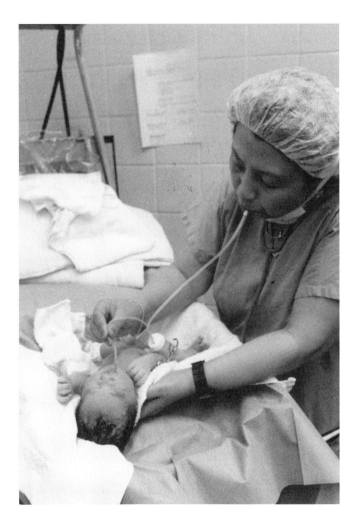

Working in the delivery room

they needed for breathing techniques and delivery. At the same time, I was available for telephone consultations and these Japanese patients began referring to me as their "New York mother." I also visited them at the hospital during my breaks, visits that were very well-received. I am proud of myself that so many mothers-to-be depended on my service and knowledge.

As my career as a Lamaze instructor took off, I was asked to write columns about birthing and raising babies in New York for New York's Japanese community newspapers such as *OCS* and the *New York Yomiuri* (later, *The Yomiuri America*). I wrote the columns for eight years, and during that time I read books written in English about child rearing. Combining the academic data and my experiences in Japan, Korea, and the United States, I realized how different child raising was between East and West, at the current time and then, in the old days. There were many things I regretted about raising my own children as I had learned to do. So, based on my mistakes, I taught these young people what I knew about parenting and the roles of wives and husbands in a developed country and I started my own newsletter, "NFC Times" (Nancy's Family Club). Unfortunately, I could not write well or teach in the Korean language; I lacked the confidence. Although I had lived longer in Korea than Japan, Japanese was my first and strongest language because I was born and raised there. Thus, I decided to begin with it first and I wrote my text in Japanese.

The most memorable class for me was one at which a husband whose leg was in a cast attended from Connecticut. The course was given over a six-week period with a roster of seven couples. This particular husband came every Sunday, walking with a crutch, his wife supporting him. He never missed a class. When I taught the method of bathing a newborn, using a doll for demonstration purposes, he stood on

Japanese Lamaze class group

Japanese gymnastic baby competition

one leg with the assistance of other fathers, trying to learn the technique with enthusiasm. Among the other students, one couple expected their second child, another were to become the parents of twins, and a third commuted a long distance, traveling more than an hour to attend my class. They asked many questions to prepare for their new babies, so the interest and attention they showed was very encouraging; I felt I wanted to do the best I could to help them. I was certain that these seven couples would become good parents and raise their children to be good human beings. In fact, I organized a gymnastic baby competition so that I could see my students again and give them an opportunity to see one another again. We all enjoyed the reunion.

Many of my students in the parenting course were elite businessmen in Japan and had been sent here by their firms. (This took place before the economic bubble burst.) Their children would be brought into a foreign world. How could I make them comfortable and confident regarding labor and childbirth? I thought it a good idea to train assistants for after-care and counseling on the phone. These activities added meaning to my middle years and a certain amount of satisfaction.

One day I was watching a video of pregnancy, labor, and child rearing in the United States, which led to the idea of making my own video in Japanese for those who could not come to my classes. It should not have been difficult to get permission from the Publicity Department to make the tape in the hospital, as I was a staff nurse in the Obstetrics Department. I could also ask parents in the classes and in the labor room to participate. I wrote a scenario, having been given a great deal of advice from my students, whose viewpoints varied. I actually made a Korean version as well.

Later, I established a non-profit organization, "Nancy *Akachan* (baby) Club" for mothers whose visa would not permit them to work in the States. I hoped the club would be a circle of Japanese women and leave them with a nice memory of New York when they returned home. I created various programs for them, making it a membership club throughout four regions, hiring educators in childcare. The members totaled as many as 300 and they all seemed to enjoy it. However, I faced a problem soon after. For some reason I became isolated from all these mothers. Why? I've never found the answer. I certainly never gained a penny from it! Perhaps it was the generation gap. Or, was it because I was Korean? Am I being paranoid? Maybe not: I did receive a letter making bigoted remarks toward my Korean background. I felt so empty—all my efforts were ignored. The *Akachan* Club was forced to close after only two years. I had to pay $4,000 in taxes from my own pocket. I laughed at the fact that I had brought it upon myself. Larry said nothing, but watched over me. Finally, he told me to "turn the page and forget it." I wish I knew how to better appreciate his kind words.

Midwives and Friends in Japan

In 1990, I attended a conference of the International Council of Midwives (ICM) in Kobe, Japan, as one of a few thousand from all over the world. It had been such a long time since I had left Japan after World War II. I went sightseeing with other midwives from New York during the breaks (this was prior to the Kobe earthquake). The monorail that ran through the city was beautiful and quiet. Passengers either read books or napped, and we were the only ones laughing and talking loudly. I think our loudness caught their attention and annoyed them. For some reason, this incident has remained in my mind.

During the conference, the Medica Company, well-known for its medical publications, held a seminar one night. I attended and was asked to speak about what I'm doing in New York hospitals. I took the microphone and spoke about my Lamaze class, *Akachan* Club, and the gymnastic baby competition. A woman raised her hand and said, "My name is Michiru Yamaguchi. I have my own practice as a midwife and I am doing the same thing under the name, *Hesono-o-kai,* The Umbilical Cord Club. She was very pleased to hear my talk and we had a chance to meet and converse later on. We hit it off right away and found that we had so much in common in terms of our careers. At the time, she was Chairperson of the Aichi Prefecture Midwife Association and she asked me to coordinate her visit to New York's labor facilities. Around then I was in the process of moving from St. Luke's-Roosevelt to St. Vincent's, a Catholic hospital. St.

Vincent's was a participating member of the Medicaid system, which allows low-income families to have the services of the OB department without charge. The patients were Korean as well as other ethnic group families, but there were also some Japanese families who were permanent residents of the United States. I chose to comply with her request since as a staff nurse, it was easy for me to arrange such a visit.

Ms. Yamaguchi came to New York the following year with seventeen other midwives to exchange ideas with their colleagues in the United States during a six-day trip. She and I built a bridge for midwives of the East and the West. I had arranged a dinner party for forty attended by this network of professionals, at which we discussed the differences between the States and Japan in the treatment of parturition. At the end of the party, all the Japanese midwives lined up shoulder-to-shoulder and sang traditional Japanese songs—and I am certain that this joyful event will remain in their memories forever. After this trip, Ms. Yamaguchi helped me on various occasions and coordinated many opportunities for my introduction of American labor care into Japan.

Speaking about American parenting to the Japanese mothers

Speaking about American parenting to the Japanese midwives

Lactation Consulting

I was surprised to learn that licensed lactation consultants were working at St. Vincent's, and I became interested in acquiring the license. Of course, it was barely a dream because my language problems persisted, so I was about to give up the idea when I discovered that a course was offered via correspondence education. I thought it might be possible to challenge it if I could study at home at my own pace, with Larry's help, of course, and I applied for "Counseling for the Nursing Mother." My instructor was a Ms. Jan Berger, who understood my struggle as a foreigner because her father had been a missionary of the Catholic Church in China. Fortunately, she exerted herself on my behalf, helping me in many ways. Her first suggestion was that I type my correspondence; thus, I bought a personal computer, which would not only force me to learn word processing, but also improve my English, and ultimately assist in the preparation for a new career. It was a matter of striking three birds with one stone.

If I were not working or seeing to domestic chores, I sat in front of the PC until late at night every night, the textbook and an English dictionary beside me. Although I attended various lactation seminars held in many locations, my level of English comprehension was probably one-tenth that of the American students. In addition to the language issue, I had a hearing loss in one ear and I couldn't see well because of my unilateral blindness. I'd begun this course thinking that I could strengthen what I had learned during my years as a professional, but it was as difficult as studying for a medical degree. We had to learn human physical and mental development, and also counseling, the function of breast-feeding, nutrition, and the chemistry of breast milk, as well as family adjustment, unique situations as the infant grew, difficulties in breast feeding, aids, techniques, etc. I had to rely on Larry's familiarity with American slang to get me through many of the terms being used.

Last day of a two-week Lactation Education program in Pennsylvania.

It took 3½ years for me to complete a two-year course. My grade, 88 points, on the formidable graduation exam was possible only because I brought my dictionary along and there was no time limit; I finally did graduate. Later, I sat my first international board exam and failed! I was very angry. The exam is called "international," but realistically, it was written for those who were fluent in English. With Larry's help, I wrote a letter of protest to the board of governors and the following year I was permitted to bring a dictionary to the exam, at which there was no longer a time restriction. Moreover, I was exempted from paying the exam fee because I'd agreed to translate the exam for future applicants when I passed it. This did not happen at the re-test. I studied for another year and was confident at my third try; however, it took me nine hours to complete the exam—a very strenuous task for a brain that was more than seventy-years old. I failed by just four points, regardless of having solved many problems of clinical technique. I regretted the failure, but took the exam again and failed again.

Jan, my instructor, said that lactation is researched more and more, "as more studies are done. At the same time, the exam will be more difficult every year." But many people were expecting that I would pass, and I felt responsible for it. Additionally, I felt a responsibility to those volunteer instructors who proctored me for the eight or nine hours of the test. So I decided to take the exam one more time, but I failed again, this time by only two points. Whenever I received notice of my failure, I felt light-headed and hadn't the stamina to stay on my feet. After a few months, my desire to sit the exam rose, but I gave it up because I believed I was too old for the license. I was seventy-four. How much longer could I practice as a lactation consultant even if I passed? When I was just about to give it up for good, I received another letter from the examination board saying that I could take the test in Japanese the following year.

I was confident of passing if the exam were in Japanese. I would no longer need to bother an instructor to attend me for many long hours. I concluded that I would do it, but as I quickly read the questions at the exam, I realized that the Japanese translation was not at all clear and was hard to understand. I'm virtually certain that an English-speaking individual translated it, but the technical terms were incorrect and seemed to have been translated with the use of an old Japanese dictionary. Unfortunately, I failed again by four points. This was failure number five. I felt so badly for those who supported me in my attempt to pass this text. Learning lactation counseling changed my attitude toward people. Yet, I often can't avoid my old self and all her insecurities rising to the surface. Looking back, I think it was a little too much for me to handle, but I don't regret that I confronted the project and I learned quite a bit. The Japanese women who took my classes in childbirth, baby care, breastfeeding preparation, and Japanese breast massage are 99% successful in their breastfeeding for about one year or more. I am now capable of solving almost all of the moms' nursing problems based on my international knowledge, techniques, and experience.

New Mother Classes

As a graduate of the CNM (Counseling Nursing Mothers) correspondence course, and as a satisfying consequence of my efforts at continuing education, I was able to reinvent my original new mothers class and write columns for Japanese community newspapers. I created the class so that young mothers could raise healthy children in the new century. There were few mothers at the beginning. Over time, however, when the importance of infant care was realized, my class gained credibility among Japanese parents, who enrolled in my hospital-authorized educational program. Now it has grown to be a noted, respected mother-baby class at St. Luke's-Roosevelt Hospital.

Dr. Takashi Eto, professor at Tokyo University's graduate school, wrote an article in the January 2002 issue of the newsletter, *"Boshi Hoken,"* ("Health for Mother and Child"). His article stated that modern children are 1) taller and more long-legged than were the older Japanese generations, although this trend would reach its limit; 2) the average strength of a child through the young adult stage has been decreasing; 3) many elementary to high school students have decayed teeth and suffer from myopia; 4) allergies in children have been increasing; and 5) recalcitrance, such as refusal to attend school, and mental issues, such as abuse, psychosomatic disorders, and nervous disorders are also increasing.

If that is the reality, I believe that modern Japan needs a structured education program for pregnancy, childbirth, lactation, and child rearing. Some geneticists subscribe to the theory that the formation of personality, body development,

201

and character are the products of environment and genetics in a ratio of 50:50. I, however, think that the percentage is 30 percent genetics and 70 percent for the living environment. There is a verified case of a girl who behaved and lived like a wolf because she had been raised by wolves, although she had been born into a healthy family. In a Russian study, the development of fifty children was examined. Half the children were raised in an orphanage where too few staff members were obliged to care for them. The remaining youngsters were raised by their own parents. This study showed a gap in the abilities of both groups by the time they were eight years of age and had started attending school. Those raised in an orphanage and had been deprived of love and attention could not perform as well in academics when compared to children with caring parents. Of course, there have been many accomplished and respected individuals who had disadvantaged childhood. Still, the Russian analysis clearly shows how great is the effect of parents' attitudes in child development.

Fortunately, we live in a time of plenty that has enabled children to grow taller than ever. However, there is a great deal of misinformation about breast feeding and bottle feeding. For a long period, mothers have used bottled milk (or packaged "formula") to feed their babies, although formula feeding was originally designed for mothers who could not provide their own breast milk. Currently, mothers tend to rely on bottled milk and formula as though they are entirely natural. As a result, children fed the latter are likely to develop more tooth decay and various allergies during their early childhood and teen years. In addition, their immune systems are likely to be compromised, making them susceptible to many diseases. A few years ago, an incident of contaminated school meals affected many children in Osaka, Japan. Some died, many were sick, and a number were unaffected. The degree of survival depended on the children's immune

With Japanese new-mother class in St. Luke's-Roosevelt Hospital

factors, no doubt. I wonder how many parents are aware that their young are quite susceptible to illness or of the considerable protective qualities of mothers' breast milk. It was because of my lactation education that I grew to realize the importance of these issues. When new mothers are misinformed or ignorant of the benefits of their breast milk, they turn to artificial food for their babies, the beginning of future health problems. Health educators should have a comprehensive view of the world and lead mothers in the right direction with practical knowledge.

Raising children while keeping pace with the rapid changes in society, one simply cannot depend on old customs handed down through the generations. It is necessary that parents educate themselves with the latest information available as soon as they become pregnant. As the nuclear family became mainstream, education for new mothers and fathers was inevitable, and such enriched educational programs will enable these parents to raise healthy, strong children, both physically and mentally. I hope that all nations will adopt these methods.

Golden Times: Supreme Happiness

I have now lived in three different countries and I consider each of them my motherland. It has been a long, harsh road, dividing my life into three phases. Ever since I left Korea without any resources, I have been able to live my life and raise my children. In the United States, I cleared two language hurdles and acquired the latest education in my field. At seventy-seven years of age, I still drive a car in mid-Manhattan, work as a healthcare professional, and teach classes on childbirth, lactation, and infant care. It is all based on my efforts and experiences throughout life. In retrospect, life has not been all bad, although it has not been all good. I have always looked ten to twenty years ahead and tried to prepare for all eventualities. One cannot make the right decision if one merely pays attention to what is immediately occurring. I believe that my long-term exertions have paid off and provided me the happiness I now enjoy with my eighty-five-year-old husband.

If I could be reborn, I would wish to be prettier and marry Larry again; but this time I would wish to marry him in our youth. I would also wish to master Japanese, Korean, and English, all as my first languages by learning them in my childhood. God must be saying, "Nancy, you want too much. I can't grant you everything. You appreciate your current happiness only because you experienced grief, only because you have endured so much hardship."

I began to write this book in hope of telling my life experiences to the younger generation. Truthfully, though, I remember my old days so clearly, including names and events, and far more pleasant occasions in the recent past I simply cannot recall. Can advanced medical technology do something about it? Perhaps not.

Lastly, I would like to share my thoughts with the readers of this book:

1. In order to solve many problems in this age of the nuclear family, we, the older generation, must awaken to realize that we can no longer depend on old customs. Encourage the young people to attend various seminars and obtain the most up-to-date education on pregnancy, childbirth, child rearing, and family life.
2. Be attentive to the cultural differences of Japan, Korea, and America.
3. There will always be a way if you make an effort to improve your life, no matter how difficult the circumstances.
4. You need to seize happiness by yourself.
5. One appreciates happiness more if one has endured hardship.
6. There should be no stinting in loving relationships. Making honest and sincere efforts to love others always compensates your loss at some point in your life.
7. In this age of the nuclear family, we should consider how to integrate the older generations with the younger to avoid a painful gap between them.
8. The future of children is dependent on the methods parents use to raise them.
9. People are born without a choice of parents or nationality. Racial discrimination is, therefore, a mirror of one's own poor-quality heart.

I hope we can all help one another by keeping these guidelines in mind, and I hope the world will become even smaller by our understanding and respect for others.

Epilogue

The Collapse of the World Trade Center: Personal Experiences

On September 11th, 2001, two passenger airplanes crashed into the World Trade Center. From my car, I saw the Twin Towers fall in a mass of smoke. I was driving on the top of a hill in New Jersey from which we can see Manhattan's tall buildings across the Hudson River. I was heading to the Lincoln Tunnel to go to Manhattan. I was alone and had no idea of what had just happened and I turned on the radio. The broadcaster was repeating that the second passenger plane had hit another tower at the WTC and there was a huge explosion. "Oh, my God!" I said as I thought about the thousands of business people who worked there. All I could do was watch the flaming Towers from across the river. Then, I realized that Larry's older sister, Helen, lives alone in an 18th floor apartment just three or four blocks away from the Trade Center. I turned and drove back to my apartment and phoned her. She didn't answer. I called Larry and he told me that his nephew, a policeman, had made sure that she was all right. Her entire building was evacuated, but Helen would not leave her apartment!

I looked at downtown Manhattan from my terrace. There, the Twin Towers that stood tall as a symbol of New York were gone. Smoke replaced the Towers. I paced back and forth between the terrace and the TV to get more news. To my knowledge, some of my students worked at the WTC, but I was unable to help and felt useless. According to TV news, four passenger planes were hijacked by terrorists simultaneously. Two hit the Trade Center, a third hit the Pentagon in Virginia, and the fourth, intended to strike the White House, crashed into the woods somewhere in Pennsylvania. On that last airplane, brave passengers who discovered the terrorists' plan fought them inside the plane and after contacting the control center, the pilot brought the plane down in the woods to deter the attack. A flight attendant on board called his wife from his cell phone and the last words he said were, "Let's go!" as he and others set upon the terrorists. This was not a scene in a film, but reality. I can't begin to imagine how his wife felt when she heard her husband's voice for the last time.

As I write this incident, tears run down my cheek. Greater damage and sacrifice were avoided by those courageous passengers and airline personnel, and the firefighters who risked their lives climbing the stairs of the WTC to rescue those who remained in the burning building. It is not possible for words to describe my deep emotion. Photos of the missing were posted later in front of the hospitals in lower Manhattan. Photos of Asians particularly caught my attention, and I found the picture of my student there. His wife called me about two weeks afterward; she said that she hadn't heard any news of her husband's whereabouts. She looked for him in every hospital in the city with little hope of his survival. As I remember, it had been less than a year since she had given birth. They lived in Battery Park City immediately adjacent to the Twin Towers and I had visited them to teach breastfeeding. He was a kind and caring husband and father. The thought of him dying in the crash, buried under a pile of debris hurt me more than the cut of a knife. I had no words to comfort her. I, too, visited hospital emergency rooms and checked the lists of WTC disaster patients, but I could not find his name anywhere. All I could do was to pray for his soul, then and now.

A French restaurant, Capsuto Frères, near Helen's apartment, was serving free food to firefighters, policemen, volunteers, and, in fact, anyone in the community for about a month. Other restaurants followed suit. America's national character was revealed in that emergency situation when each helped the other. The American flag was seen everywhere, many on cars, including my own. Subsequent to the tragedy, I spoke with Mr. Nakano and his wife and my sister-in-law Helen.

Helen: I heard a big explosion and said to my dog, Yogi, "What was that sound?" and looked out the window. Oh, my God! The top of the North Tower was blazing and black smoke poured from it. And white things, many of them, were falling out of the windows. Then I saw a second plane fly in and in and hit the South Tower at its side. There was another explosion and the South Tower collapsed in no time. I learned later that the white things falling from the windows were people.

Nancy: Your building was evacuated after that. But you didn't leave your apartment. Why?

Helen: They didn't allow us to take our pets. I didn't want to leave my dog, Yogi. Even if I died there, I was 88 years old. I had no regrets. My apartment was covered with white dust. I kept cleaning it off, but nothing was enough to get rid of the dust. So I had a sore throat. But doctors and nurses came to the building every day to check on those who weren't evacuated. We were also brought three meals a day. They were so helpful.

Nancy: Mr. Nakano, you live in Battery Park City right next to the WTC. Can you tell me what it was like?

Mr. Nakano: I drank too much the night before. But I woke up at 8:30 A.M. and walked over to the Trade Center

211

as usual and got my coffee. My office is in the tall building along the East River, facing west. I was contacting the Tokyo office as I always did, when the American staff members said, "Oh shit," and began to make noise. They told me that either an American or United airplane crashed, or something. I wasn't aware of terrorism at the time. I thought that a beginner pilot made a mistake and crashed. But it was immediately after the crash that papers were covering the sky. I realized that a terrible accident had happened. I rushed to the phone to contact Tokyo again. Then a call came in from a staff member in the Tokyo office who was watching TV. He told me that a second plane crashed into another building. I looked out the window and found the South Tower had been hit. The area was covered with smoke and paper. I thought it was strange that two planes would crash into buildings, one after the other. It was only then I thought about the possibility of terrorism. I turned on a small TV in the office. It was around the time that many people arrived at the office for work, but I directed that the personnel office evacuate everyone and send them home.

Nancy: Where was your wife Keiko then?

Mr. Nakano: She left home at 7:00 A.M. to go to the English school in Midtown. So I was sure she was OK, but I was worried about my apartment. I called my wife's family in Japan to tell them Keiko was in a safe area and I left the office. There were many ambulances and fire trucks on the street. In addition, ordinary people as well as professionals were taking photographs and videos. It was impossible to go through Broadway, so I walked on the West Side Highway, which was also closed, but I walked there anyhow. I saw a tire so huge I had never seen one like it and I realized it was an airplane tire. As I walked, I wondered where we could spend the night. Fortunately, my apartment was not damaged. When I was about to sit down to calm myself, I heard a roaring sound like an earthquake from outside. I wasn't sure what happened. I looked out the window as I thought that a third plane might have attacked somewhere. My apartment faces the WTC. Enormous billows of smoke, just like from a volcano, were blowing toward me and I saw people running on the ground. Smoke continued toward me and our 19th floor apartment windows were covered with smoke. It was like being at the bottom of a muddy river. I didn't know what to do but I took the elevator, which was still running, down to the lobby. People who were outside rushed into my building to avoid smoke, and everyone, both men and women, were crying. Outside, it was dark and the air smelled bad. I still didn't know what had happened but was able to go outside when the smoke cleared a little. It was still filled with smoke, of course; nevertheless I tried to walk up along the Hudson River to return to my office. As I walked, I heard another roaring sound, but didn't know that both the Twin Towers had collapsed. I couldn't see a thing through the smoke.

Nancy: Was your office damaged?

Mr. Nakano: Fortunately my office was OK. That's why I wanted to get back there somehow.

Nancy: How far is your office from your apartment?

Mr. Nakano: It usually takes fifteen minutes on foot, but it took an hour that day. I walked to Wall Street, which has an open and direct view, but the smoke still prevented me from seeing the area. Everyone was covered with dust. I reached my office on the 26th floor, but only my boss was there. He didn't know what happened either, so we called the London office and they told us that the Twin Towers had collapsed.

Nancy: What kind of business is your company in?

Mr. Nakano: It's an investment consulting firm. Anyway, at the office, we received many calls from the families of our employees. I told them that everyone had been evacuated. Finally, my wife phoned and I told her not to come home. I suggested she kill some time at Starbucks or the like, and was very relieved that she was safe.

Nancy: What were you doing, Keiko?

Keiko: I was taking a class at 8:00 A.M. in midtown. I was glad it was out of the immediate area.

Nancy: Were you pregnant?

Keiko: No, I wasn't. I was going to the English school next to the Empire State Building. My class was 8:00 to 10:00 A.M., but before 10:00, a teacher told us that the school was closing and she had us leave the building. They didn't tell us any of the reasons. I went to the subway station, but the train didn't come for an hour. Then we heard an announcement telling us to leave the station because the trains were not running. I got out anyway and saw women crying and ambulances everywhere. I realized that something had happened. Someone said that something had happened in the WTC and I didn't like the news because I lived right next to it. I then waited for a bus, which was very crowded—actually I had to wait for the third bus to get on. I asked another passenger what happened and she told me that the Trade Center was hit by planes and collapsed. "What was she talking about?" I thought. I believed she was teasing me because I didn't speak much English. The bus didn't go any further than 14th Street. I said that I was going home to Battery Park City, and she said, "You won't be able to go home. Go to the library or something or call your family." My husband then told me to go to a Starbucks, but none of the shops were open. So I started walking south to go home as everyone else was walking north.

A policeman screamed at me not to enter the area, but I said that I wanted to go to my home in Battery Park City. Again, the policeman screamed, "Are you going to go where thousands of people are dying?" For the first time, I realized something terrible had happened. I had no idea what to do, so I called my husband again. He said that I needed to go uptown to the home of the company's president. I had nothing with me but a notebook and textbook. I bought a toothbrush and underwear on the way to that apartment. I stayed there about two weeks. After ten or so days, I heard the news that Battery Park City residents could go home with ID, but I didn't have my passport or a driver's license, so I brought the proof of address issued by my school. The military officers didn't trust me although I told them that as a foreigner I was not eligible for a driver's license. After a while, an officer accompanied me to my apartment.

Nancy: Could your apartment key be considered proof?

Keiko: No. They said anyone could make a copy anywhere. They were suspicious to the end. I couldn't take much time because the officer was waiting. I took my passport and left. Security was so tight. The second time I went back there, even my passport was no longer sufficient ID. (There was more conversation which I have omitted.)

During my lifetime I have experienced three great cataclysms, two in the Twentieth century: the Asian theater of the Second World War, where the first nuclear tragedy took place; and the Korean conflict, with repercussions even today; and the third as the twenty-first century began: the destruction of New York's World Trade Center, which has set the United States on a dark and perilous path. I was only one person among hundreds of thousands affected by each of these episodes of madness and I survived as witness to the violence our fellow human beings have inflicted and continue to inflict. Before September 11, 2001, I optimistically believed that my older years would never again observe such upheavals—certainly never on my beloved America's soil. Sixty-five years—a lifetime in itself—have passed, but Hiroshima, the war in Korea, and the recent Twin Towers attack remain vividly in my thoughts.

Throughout this book, I have tried to bring the reader a view of one small human life enmeshed in a daily struggle of survival on both the individual level and also amid the events of world conflict. If I have given eminence to my past, I would consider this memoir a success.

Appendix I: The Atomic Bomb at Hiroshima and Me

By Minoru Fujii, MD, Former President of the National Veterans Hiroshima Sanitarium Hospital

A Record of Relief Activities for Radiation Sickness Caused by the Atomic Bomb at Hiroshima City

Dr. Minoru Fujii

On August 6, 1945, I had to arrange for a relief party after the Atomic Bomb was dropped two hours earlier. At that time, I was the President of the National Hiroshima Sanitarium Hospital. About 10:00 o'clock in the morning, I was informed by the police department that I needed to mobilize my department for relief services in Hiroshima City. Immediately, I formed the first group of relief workers, ten people with group leader surgeon Sawasaki. When I received their report I realized it was a grave situation. Soon I made up the second group including me; I remember it was about 4:00 P.M. I will write the details of those miserable conditions later. Anyway, we used piped water from the eastern district and the police department assisted in the relief activities while, until 8:00 P.M., we attended to the burns of about seventy victims suffering with radiation and other injuries.

August 7: I sent two more relief groups to the affected area. The first group of doctors and nurses remained to care for the in-patient victims. After that, I alternated doctors and sent them out in a two-to-three-days rotation.

August 8: Our group went to the Motokawa Elementary School. There, we found naked bodies lying at the school gates. Some survivors were barely able to move when they heard our voices. Inside the gates, a volunteer group from Seragun, about ten people, just wandered around, not knowing what to do. For the time being, we moved the survivors to the classrooms, However, the most logical area to accommodate the patients was the floor of the burned building, although it was now uneven, and there were neither mats nor covers for sick and injured. Some survivors complained of the cold, but we had no way to help. Fortunately, after a while someone was able to bring straw mats and we at least had something to use as blankets. First, we tried to give ID tags to those we moved, but some hesitated to wear them. Our treatment for the wounds was only sterilization with Mercurochrome, application of zinc oxide oil for burns, and then wrapping the wounds with sterilized garments that had been disposed of. I was uncertain that such treatment would be satisfactory and constantly worried about the results. After that, I took part in relief activities at a few other areas where neither the patients nor their treatment varied.

The Condition and Symptoms of Radiation Sickness Caused by the Atomic Bomb

As I drove to Hiroshima City in the afternoon of August 6, I saw so many, many people whose burnt clothing and skin hung from their bodies. In Kaita, they wandered around like ghosts so that I could scarcely catch my breath observing them. After Kyoubridge, we found the people on the streets in extremely miserable condition and barely able to speak. "Water! Water!" they pleaded; it still remains in my ears. When I think back, I feel very badly not knowing which was the most meaningful, the water I gave those people or the treatment at the Eastern District Police Department. I do not have the words to describe the condition and symptoms of the victims; my literary talent is poor, but I can say that if someone seems to overstate or paint a horrific verbal picture, it is not exaggerated. I am ashamed to say that my sensibilities soon became numb. When I saw the victims for the first time, I lost my head completely, but I had to harden my heart, and after a short time in the city, I was becoming accustomed to it. Even when seriously affected victims on the street wanted water, I ignored them and continued on to my destination. I felt as though my own humanity were deteriorating as well. My mission lay in relief administration. A proverb says that a hunter does not see the mountain. We concentrated on our efforts to find the first aid station and to apply the proper treatment (as far as was possible) to the victims. I think we had no inner resources left to react to the horrible sights and I fell into a deep depression.

Shock and Misapprehension Among the Victims

We interviewed more than two hundred victims who had suffered from the bomb, some who were in-patients, and

219

some who were treated at out-patient clinics. However, wonderfully, nobody remembered what happened! Only one person, living nearby in Matoba, said that the event had been hot!! Almost everyone lay on the ground face-forward at the time of explosion. Someone called out that an incendiary bomb had been dropped. I realized that when an occurrence such as this huge disaster takes place, our perceptions become numb.

Discovery of Radiation Sickness (Acute Decremental Granulocytic Leukopenia)

I think that around August 9th during a meeting of relief coordinators, I heard about a serious patient with radiation sickness in Iwakuni Kure Navy Hospital who had been diagnosed with acute decremental granulocytic leukopenia. I was interested and requested blood tests of the thermal burn victims in our hospital, too, finding the samples not any different from those studied at Kure. I ordered continuing observation of these patients. Dr. Hiroshi Shirai, a colleague, had a special interest in these cases. At the time, I lived in an official residence in our hospital and the Director of Pharmacy, Kota Yoshitomi, also lived close with his family. His adolescent son, Ken, a fine student, was caught in Hiroshima when the bomb was dropped, but escaped injury beneath a building.

Of course when he returned home safely all his family was so delighted. However, it was afterward that he began to feel off-color and complained of weakness and nausea. Dr. Shirai performed a blood test. Six days after the attack Ken's white-blood-cell count was 4000 so that he was quickly put on bed-rest. Finally, on August 18th he had a high fever and when Dr. Shirai checked his white cell count it had dropped to 300. Blood transfusions and other protocols were immediately administered, but he died on August 27. His last words were, " . . . how bitterly disappointing it was that General MacArthur ever came to Japan."

When Dr. Shirai's reports indicated that uninjured patients were exhibiting decreases in their white count, we decided to initiate a research project into radiation sickness immediately (August 19). We contacted the Saijo Police Department and the town hall to provide everything necessary for full-scale blood testing of our in-patient and out-patient clinic. We decided to admit anyone found with a decreased white-blood-cell count. As many as 77 patients were admitted one after another. Furthermore, we requested that the newspaper print an announcement and a warning, but unfortunately, the Saijo newspaper staff had been evacuated and the equipment was no longer operational. Finally, at the beginning of September, a notice was published.

In the meantime, the illness, *Acute Decremental Granulocytic Leukopenia*, had been defined in an announcement by Dr. Totsuki on Mainichi News in Tokyo at the end of August. It was a real disappointment because our team had already discovered it and had admitted and treated many patients to whom we were devoted. The result of our research about radiation sickness, ADGL, appeared in the journal of the Science Council of Japan, *Nippon Gakujutsu Sinkokaikanko* in 1953.

Some Musings on the War and the A Bomb

For more than forty years following World War II, there are some people who are still criticizing U.S. action and crying out against the misery and damage it inflicted. They say that the dropping of the A bomb was inhuman, and they have urged the establishment of an antiwar movement. It seems understandable, but it is not clearly understandable to me. I also felt we were completely taken in by America. I think such beliefs are a natural post-war public sentiment. The sense of defeat prevailed. My recollection of that period was that all Japanese were combatants, men and women trained to use bamboo spears for war.

When we began relief activities that first day, we found many eye injuries among the police that had been caused by smoke and flames while the officers attempted to quell the fires that were rampant. I chanced upon the Public Prosecutor, Mr. Tsunoda, who said that his family was gone, "I now feel free to fight in Japan's proper war."

There is a written record in the archives of Hiroshima University, "Victims' Radiation Sickness Caused by the Atomic Bomb," titled, "The Death of Professor Ri Ichi Takenaka," a statement taken at his bedside. "The enemy used splendid tactics," he said. "The A Bomb was another weapon. What is the use of complaining after we lost the war?"

No matter how long there are protests against nuclear weapons, the weapons will remain until replaced by another "valuable" device.

Translated by Nancy Cantwell

Appendix II: Under Mushroom Clouds

By Akiko Sakamaki*

My Aunt

I had an Aunt Okei and Uncle Gorozo.
They were lovely people to me.
They had a small business in an upstream village.
They were just about to evacuate with their belongings to a
    place of safety.
Then!—Lightening shot down and Bam!!—
They were groaning in a smashed house.
Okei barely crawled out of the crushed house.
She called her husband's name desperately.
"Help! Help me!" Gorozo said from inside the house.
The house burst into flame.
Outside, the grandparents were choking.
"Go! Go! Everybody! I'll stay with Gorozo."
"I don't want to leave him alone."
Okei was running into the flames.
Grandmother watched them being consumed, Okei's body
    virtually atop Gorozo.

Translated by Nancy Cantwell

---

* Ms. Akiko was a Japanese nurse, a colleague of Nancy Cantwell.

Appendix III: Voices of Korean War Victims

Many long years later, I led a discussion of Korean War experiences with three of my Korean friends as I had with my Japanese companions. The participants were Ms. Kang Fungsung, Ms. Kim Chonghi, and Ms. Kim Ouc.

Nancy: Where were you when the incident of June 25th took place?

Kang: I was probably in the third grade of middle school, but I don't remember it clearly. My family was evacuated to Oryudong, a small village far from Seoul, and I commuted from the village to the Yongdungpo school in Seoul. After all the important government officials were evacuated, the Hang Gan Bridge entering Seoul was destroyed, so the transportation system was in chaos. I sometimes took a ferry to school, or if I was lucky, I would hitchhike and get a lift in a truck. With all this difficulty, I still managed to go to school every day. One day, I was able to take a train, and felt very lucky. Lucky, that is, until the train had an accident and I was badly injured. The injuries included a complete loss of memory: I could recall nothing of my life before the derailment.

Nancy: Have any of your childhood memories been recovered?

Kang: No, they haven't. I was just so relieved to come home when Seoul was returned to Korea on September 28th.

Kim C.: I didn't have too much of a bad time during the war because my father was president of a Korean gunpowder mill. But when the northern army suddenly attacked us, all of my family were separated. I tried to escape with my mother, loading as much luggage and household goods as was possible on a wagon and dragging it out on the street. There were so many people with so many of their possessions, all walking very briskly. We weren't sure where they were heading, but we followed along anyway. When we reached Nundamun market, we found it empty. With the Hang Gan Bridge destroyed, we had no idea of how to proceed, and then, as we walked back and forth, someone screamed out that a North Korean tank was approaching. We ran and ran, until a red-flagged tank stopped in front of us. I was really scared, but a small boy about fifteen or sixteen years old, popped out of the tank, and the boy shouted, "We won't shoot if you clap your hands!" So, we clapped our hands! His face still looked innocent: like a young farmer who was trained for just a few days of warfare. It is so sad that we had to kill one another and boys of that tender age had to be dragged out. (She wept.)

After a while, my mother and I were able to see other members of our family, including all the employees at the mill. My father was responsible for about fifty mill workers, and I recall my mother worrying about a rice shortage with all those people to be fed. All the rice stores were closed, refusing to sell it. The North Korean army somehow knew that my family had some rice and demanded it from my mother at gunpoint. She answered that we were short of rice also and that they should be giving some to us if they had it! Other than these conditions, I don't remember serious deprivation.

Kim O.: They knew which family had what.

Kang: I wonder how they got their information. But they were better than the Russian army. I heard that many women were raped by the Russians. We were lucky, in a way.

Nancy: How about you, Kim?

225

Kim O.: I was also in the third grade of middle school. I was swimming at school with some classmates when my teacher rushed to the pool and ordered us to go home because war had broken out. None of us took it seriously because we thought it was the teacher's excuse to make us leave quickly.

Kim C.: You had a swimming pool at your school?

Kim O.: Yes, we did. After a while, we realized that our teacher was not joking. We went home as quickly as possible. My mother was there waiting for me, but her face had no color and she was trembling with fear. My father was a policeman, so if we were caught by the North Korean army, we would be killed immediately. I followed my mother to a house in the mountains to hide, but to remain hidden, we couldn't use a light after nightfall, so we pulled the light bulb to the floor, covering it with a black umbrella as a precaution. I never forgot that.

Kang: I felt so sorry for the families of policemen.

Kim O.: Not long after, we were called by the school, but my relatives suggested that we be evacuated to a safer location. So many people had so many different ideas and we felt so lost. At last, my family decided that the North Koreans would not mistreat children, so while my older sister went to school, we prepared our belongings and moved away to my mother's parents' house in the countryside. (There was more conversation which I have omitted.)

In retrospect, although the war years were difficult for them, it seems to me that these women's experiences were mild, when compared to the deaths and dreadful privation of so many others I had observed.

Appendix IV: Letter from Dr. Minoru Fujii

January 20, 1987
Dear Mrs. Nancy Cantwell,
   I read your recent letter with amusement and appreciation. It has been a long time since I heard from you, but this letter was filled with joy and happiness. You have played your role on the stage of life with such passion and enthusiasm. It is a great ending for both player and audience. They say that reality is stranger than fiction. Your life is just like this expression. Congratulations. I always believed that life is created with faith and effort. You have proved my belief. I wish I kept your letters from Korea. They were the hard days of your life and I am so happy for your happiness in America.
   I was also delighted to hear of your success in teaching of the Lamaze. I think it is because of your passion and courage.
   Your writing of Japanese has also improved. I wonder if it is because of your job. I am so proud of you.
   I am amazed how well your son Heamin and daughter Yusun grew up. Their mother must have led them in the right direction, I wish you the best. Please take care of yourself.

Sincerely,
Minoru Fujii (Former Director of the Nursing School)

Appendix V: Principles of Western Child Care

I am so sorry that I didn't know of Western child-raising principles when my own children were infants, but here are those I have learned in the States since then, and what I teach my students.

1. Parents give life to their offspring, but children are individual human beings with their own rights.
2. Children are not parents' belongings. They should not be forced to do only the parents' bidding.

- Raising children starts from accepting the child's humanity and need for a great deal of love.
- Child-rearing is based on the recognition of the individual. Each child is unique and develops his or her intellectual and physical talents at his or her own pace. Parents need to be aware that siblings most often vary in development. Flexibility is desirable and a youngster should be allowed some freedom while they are being trained.
- Children need to learn to think for themselves.
- Children need encouragement in order to develop autonomy and the will to study, work, and play.
- Physical and intellectual training are equally important. Children should be encouraged to experience a variety of ideas and activities because they learn through their experiences.
- Parents and, in fact, all adults, should try to make childhood enjoyable and loving.

- We must lead children in preparing themselves for the future as they pass through everyday life.
- We need to train offspring to live in society, think logically, and work responsibly.

3. Parents are the older generation and are responsible for teaching their young the skills of survival.

- We need to look after their well-being and tend them when they are ill.
- We need to be good counselors and support our young mentally and physically.
- Our children need to be praised for their accomplishments as frequently as possible to develop their self-confidence.
- We must raise our youngsters to feel comfortable enough to speak with us if they have a problem.
- We should not force a child to answer our questions.
- We need to allow the child to resolve an issue for himself or herself rather than do it for them.
- Children appreciate sharing our own experiences of either success or failure.